Mud and Dreams

Mud and Dreams

*Essays on Falling
More Deeply in Love with Life*

JOHN SEAN DOYLE

Rainstick Press, Raleigh, NC
2018

Grateful acknowledgment is made to Samy Briss, for permission to use an image of his work, *Shabbat,* on the cover. Thanks also to Allison J. Doyle for permission to use her photo of the author on the back cover.

ISBN-13: 978-1-7322285-0-4

First Printing: 2018

Rainstick Press
4006 Barrett Drive #104
Raleigh, North Carolina 27609
Attn: J. Doyle
www.JohnSeanDoyle.com

Ordering Information:

For all inquiries, please contact the author at LiveFully@JohnSeanDoyle.com. Special discounts are available on quantity purchases by corporations, associations, educators, and others.

Front and back cover design by John H. Moore, jhmoore.com

For Jenny, Andrieu, Abigail and Allison.

If I could give you anything, it would be the clarity and calm
to always see the hope, beauty and goodness
that is around you every day.

What a strange machine man is! You fill him with bread, wine, fish, and radishes, and out comes sighs, laughter, and dreams.

- Nikos Kazantzakis

Contents

Introduction: The Hard and Beautiful Task of Being Human

I used to love to play in the rain. There was an old, dry ditch in the back of the yard, cracked and quiet, usually unnoticed. When the rains fell, it came alive: exuberant; effervescent; howling with memories of The Great Flood and dreaming it were one of history's holy rivers. I would linger on its new born banks and walk and splash within its swells. In the driveway and yard, puddles emerged everywhere. And as the drops fell from heaven and cloud, I caught them on my tongue and let soak their secrets. Head thrown back, encumbrances gone, the universe would dowse me with everything she had to offer.

I was always surprised, I am still surprised, when people would say it was a "bad day" because it is overcast or raining.

I passionately believe there is beauty all around us and reason for hope. I am confirmed in my faith, again and again, in the goodness of people, and that we have at our finger tips, access to so much meaning and promise, if we would only let ourselves see.

Yet so often, it is so hard to see. Turn on the news and we cannot avoid everything that is wrong with the world. There is a growing anger and hostility. We have lost faith in media and government, big business and the church. Everywhere it is the politics of cynical self-interest and vindictiveness, an ethos of convenience and negligent disregard. There are the challenges of work and parenting and living with the changing people we love. There are bills to pay and mold in the crawl space. Health issues disrupt everything we had planned, and we have lost touch with our dreams. And meanwhile somewhere far away, but still too close, other people's sons and daughters are consigned to grizzled sub-genres of history where there is no charity. People's lives are filled with a poetry that has nothing to do with words.

How are we to live in such a world? How do we reconcile all the joy and grandeur and wonder that really do exist, with the heart-ripping pains and traumas, the losses and the fears that wake us at night? How do we learn to embrace everything that is within our grasp, yet out of our control, so that life becomes something more than managing the whims of a fickle and indifferent universe? How do we live lives of radical amazement and joy, so they become an intimate celebration of the whole of being?

We can leaf through the pages of the sacred texts. We can wring beautiful truths from antiquity's scrolls, or even plot what science has taught on distribution curves. However, sometimes what we want and need and long for is simple validation of where we are in the struggle. To be given hope and reasons to hope. To be assured that while the things of life can be hard, difficult, scary, irrational, unjust and unfair; that fundamentally there is no reason to fear or fret or fade. To recognize that there is always, always just-cause to love life and to celebrate the tender, rapturous, beautiful intimacies that also are our inheritance. We are not the first ones in this world to suffer or struggle or doubt. We won't be the last. And there is comfort in knowing we never need go it alone.

Mud and Dreams is a series of essays and stories on the poetry and science of living. It is *poetic non-fiction* about recovering a reverence for being. The essays touch some of the most fundamental human concerns, such as Truth, Beauty, Kindness, Hope, Resilience, Gratefulness and the Sacred.

At times lyrical, at times pragmatic, each poem-essay can be read independently or in any order. They are short enough to be consumed anywhere life happens; waiting in airports, or on the subway. However, if you read them in order, you might discover a thread running through them, connecting us back to a vision of a world that is rich and whole and hopeful. In addition, in the *Afterword*, I have included prompts, thoughts and exercises for each essay to work through independently, or with loved ones or book clubs, to help build deeper connections.

As you read *Mud and Dreams*, dog-ear the pages. Scribble notes in the margins. Fold the readings into your life and create something personal and meaningful. My hope is that over the months and years you will continue to come back to these pages, and that the words will meet you wherever you are. That as you lift the book from the shelf, it will speak to you again and again in ways that are comfortable and familiar, or comfortable and new. If I am lucky, occasionally these dream-songs might stumble across something that resembles what it means to live the world, beautifully and passionately, and with honesty, integrity and grace.

I want you to believe in fairy tales again. I want you to believe in the goodness of people, that there is beauty all around us, and that there is reason for hope. I want you to know that you are better than you thought you were. If I can offer anything, let it be a little more promise and joy, that you both become softer, and recognize your strength. May you always find things for which you are grateful, and that your life be filled with heart-rich and meaningful connections. In the end, what I want, is that you can look upon your life and fall even more deeply in love with the world.

Gratefully,

Sean Doyle
January 17, 2018
Raleigh, NC

Part I. Living in the World

Sinkholes

I first heard about sinkholes when I was six years old. Mrs. Flood, my teacher, explained how through erosion or a broken water main, the bedrock supporting our roadways, parking lots and backyards could be silently washed away until the ground collapsed, taking with it cars, swing sets, or even our homes. I was gripped with terror.

She explained how sinkholes occurred. Our textbook offered proof in photographs. But we never discussed how to live in a world where the very ground upon which we stood could, without notice, open up beneath our feet.

How are we to live our lives? This is the question we come back to again and again. Some version of it is at the heart of every play by Shakespeare, every poem by Whitman, Milosz and Homer. It is the question probed by philosophers and psychologists. It is writ in the ancient languages of our sacred texts and is lived by every lawyer and businessmen; farmer and theologian; day laborer and house keeper. Turning page after page in the solitude of our study, some of us are so overcome by the question we cut off anything that resembles a real life. Our "answer" becomes contemplation. Many of us are content to go through life with no need to ask or think or question at all. We simply let the response choose itself through the fog of our actions and inactions and the destinies we walk away from.

And then one day something changes: An acquaintance or loved one dies; we are diagnosed with cancer; or some other metaphorical sinkhole opens in the center of our world.

The change could be one of the many miracles of life: the birth of a child; the falling in love; the coming together of so many disconnected things. Time and again, as if in accordance with some unwritten script, life nudges us awake from our decades-long sleepwalk. We wipe the gum from our eyes and ask: "*Is this all there is?*"; "*Could there be something more?*"; "*What am I to do with this life?*".

It is a question of meaning. It is a question of happiness. It is a pragmatic question of ethics and choice. When reduced to words we talk about purpose and value, efficacy and self-worth. In the middle of our everyday, we seek coherence and go about connecting the disparate things. We pursue our dreams, live rich, enjoyable lives and maintain a commitment to responsible action. At times, life even unreasonably demands that we reassess those very things upon which we've rested everything. And through it all, despite whatever has happened and regardless of what we have been told, we know as surely as an infant finds sanctuary and promise in her mother's gaze, that the answer involves kindness, acceptance and gratitude.

To flourish is not just positive emotions and the yellow, smiling stickers handed out by first grade teachers like Mrs. Flood. It is that experience of being wholly alive, of being intimately engaged in life. It is being able to fully participate in all aspects of being human: the physical; mental; relational. We are communal animals. We lead rich psychological and emotional lives. We create whole cultures, and live certain spiritual truths that cannot be measured or explained in ways that make any real sense. Flourishing might be expressed as boisterous effervescence and lived out loud and in the open. It might be marked by calm, contentment and an "inner~vescence" that is invisible to the voyeurs who would crowd our lives. To live completely is a felt poetic.

To participate fully is not about accomplishment. It does not mean that we must be pain free or graceful or perfect in what we do. Rather it is about immersing yourself in life and rediscovering the world as wholly new and alive. It is looking upon everything around you with freshness and appreciation, gratitude and wonder. It is about being curious and allowing yourself to be touched; because there is so much that depends on you. So much that is subtle and good and beautiful and all around us if we only take the time to notice. Savor the foods you eat. Smile at that ache in your knee as you feel the holiness that is your body in motion. Marvel at wild mushrooms and that your baby girl has become a woman. And if you can, give yourself over to something bigger, to something you can never change: By so doing, you do affect change. Flourishing is about immersing yourself in the magnificence of others and finding that you care for another more than you do for yourself. To be fully alive is to allow yourself to dance, to laugh, to let the tears well up in your eyes when you are touched or saddened. It means living lives of "affective prosperity" ~ to embrace

9

all of the authentic emotions and feelings that make us fully human and alive and that add a texture and richness to life.

What of the hardships and traumas that so rudely force themselves upon us? What of the feelings that bring us pain? There is truth in that Buddhist notion that pain is inevitable, but suffering is not. But be careful with even the greatest of truths.

The way we think about the world, the way we interpret the events of our lives, very well may contribute to all of our joys and sufferings. When the hurt hurts too much, there is the persistent temptation to disconnect from the world, to inhale only detached observations, or wrap ourselves up so tightly that we no longer feel.

And who am I to say to anyone who has felt pain that they should not disconnect? There is a danger to being sensitive to the world. Who am I to say that they should not do whatever it takes to alleviate their suffering? The hardest thing in life may be to stand there, naked and exposed and accept injustices and indiscretions like the burning of the sun.

But there is an honesty in allowing ourselves to be open. And where we are honest, truths appear. To be fully alive means to lay ourselves out in the open, vulnerable to a detached universe, and allow ourselves to experience life's deep, nurturing joys, as well as its inevitable pains. Living to neither shut ourselves off from those things that make life difficult, nor to allow the cataracts of habit to blind us to the miracles and goodness that are around us all the time. There is an unrivaled intimacy to being sensitive to the truths of the world. When we feel them, our hearts beat in rhythm with every pulse of every star.

With each inhalation and exhalation, our breath assumes the constancy of the sea. When we allow ourselves to be open and sensitive to the world, we become an integral part of that world. We ourselves become more human, more complete.

To flourish is not about unrelenting bliss or freedom from pain and injustice. One can live a life of meaning, significance and value even when feeling empty. Your life can be something good and powerful and world-altering, despite suffocating under despair. We are always affecting others. We never know the extent of that impact. Whether you recognize it or not, your life matters. Even if you have made some big mistakes, suffered some terrible trauma, or have regrets that cut to the very heart of your being: you can still offer the hope and promise and decency every one of us needs. In fact, you may be in a better position to do so, precisely because you know what it means to have struggled or been in pain. Please be good for the world. You are too important not to.

And the most wonderful part of it all, is that it is all, always changing. There is not one among us who is perfect or stagnant. We are always becoming. Chance or fate or some other god is always mixing the expected and unexpected, handing us something new, and inviting us to shape our lives all over again. We are asked to find beauty and truth and love and hope again and again. At times, this feels like a reason to despair. After we have worked so hard, overcome so much, we watch helplessly as a sinkhole opens and swallows everything we've built and relied upon. But if we are patient and grateful, our breath will find its natural grace. Each inhalation will freshen us, as is the purpose of breath. The beauty we uncover, yesterday's successes, the triumphs of goodness, are all the proof we need: We are *essential* for assuring that this world is wondrous, miraculous and good. And when the traumas do come, let yourself feel them. But then, let it them go. They are over. They never were what mattered. When the sunlight peaks over that line of horizon, we get to start over again too.

We are most ourselves, the most human, when we unabashedly immerse ourselves in the world with love and hope, gratitude and kindness. Sometimes it is as easy as cherry blossoms falling on your shoulders and in your hair. Other times we have to grab life with both hands, and twist and squeeze and wrench just to extract one sweet drop from this world: But oh how sweet, how nourishing and wholesome, when we discover that even a drop of joy and beauty and hope is possible.

Horizons

I don't know the purpose of the sunrise. As I lay on the beach looking out over the water, I can't say anything about indubitable truths or universal structures of knowledge. I only know to look for the foundations of meaning in the lived experience of the world.

The sun coming up over the seascape hints at something beyond ourselves. Everything I know and see, everything I feel with my heart and head, is ringed by that minuscule bubble of horizon. Yet the horizon points past itself to what lay outside of awareness, outside of direct perception, and to a world of anticipation, hope and expectation. That is the world in which we live – one part perception, another part assumption and longing.

You walk into a coffee shop or party and are thrilled and nervous at seeing the woman that you've long been drawn to, but have been too shy to approach. Her back is to you. You recognize her friends, and the way her hair flows down her back. With a dry mouth and lump in the throat you find the courage to approach, tap her on the shoulder and are surprised and disappointed when someone unknown to you turns.

Our views of things are always inherently incomplete. Philosopher Maurice Merleau-Ponty explains that every aspect of a thing is only an invitation to perceive beyond it.[1] The dress. The heels. A familiar hairstyle and some common friends. They all pointed toward an expectation of the woman you wanted to see. The "horizon" of our perception delimits our perspective. It is anticipation that leads us out beyond the boundaries. And so, our experience of the world is more than our perception. Edmund Husserl explains everything that "is", every "actuality", also involves its potentialities.[2] Everything I see refers to something anticipated, but not yet perceived.

Of course, horizons are not limited to the visual plane. When I was lying on the beach, the salt breeze carried with it the sweetness of lemon blossoms and a hint of the sour rot of fish. There are smells beyond smells. A gull called to me over the gentle hush of surf. There are sounds beyond sounds. I tasted salt from the sea and felt the sun warming my skin. Everything we see, hear, smell, feel and taste is demarked by its own horizon.

There are also cultural and psychosocial horizons. Every star by which we set our bearings is hung within the limits of awareness. We have beliefs about the world and what we want it to be. We hold tightly to our notions of justice or fairness. We want to believe the stories our parents told us as children, the fairy tales, the sacred texts. We believe that goodness matters, that humility and integrity have a "cash value"[3] after all, and that with persistence and grit and kindness, dreams do come true. Yet we do our jobs with diligence and integrity and go unnoticed. We are surprised at how often the people we thought were there for us, let us down. We expect that the ladies in big houses don't need the refuge of a women's shelters. Except sometimes they do. Ivy League graduates do not become alcoholics. Children who are deprived of all companionship and love are fated to spend the rest of their lives struggling to pick up the pieces, except when they show they are the strongest among us; except when they illuminate the very best of the human spirit and act as the pillars upon which community rests.

We have beliefs about who we ourselves are too. Yet sometimes we push through a hardship or rough spot and discover that we are better than we thought we were. At times the beliefs we hold about others are challenged, when someone close to us betrays our trust, or lets us down, because they are more human than we wanted to let them be.

Life sometimes has its own plan. It happens with its own logic, its own pace. The universe has no regard for what we wanted or had come to expect. You defined your life in terms of activity and strength and then are nearly crippled by chronic knee pain in early adulthood. Or you invested in real estate to pay for college for the kids, only to have the bottom drop out of the housing market. Or one day you discover a silent tumor whispering to you in the Latin of Stoics and altar boys, *memento mori,* and you realize that the appointments you have written on the calendar might never come. We are Alice falling down the rabbit hole. It is as if one of the mischievous gods from another era had come down to visit and played some trick. We can shake our head at the injustice, eyes turned down. We can lift our fist to the sky and scream. Or, soaked in these new facts about our world, we can throw our arms wide, *dash with our hair,*[4] and joyously embrace the next hardship or adventure life hands us. Absurdity is never out of place. Nothing is ironic or paradoxical. It is simply a matter of expecting something different than what lay beyond the horizon.

Why does any of this matter? Certainly, we see in Husserl the first steps toward modern studies in affective forecasting.[5] We draw on clues from experience, perception and memory and try to predict what might make us happy. Social psychologists examine how the unseen influences our lives. Priests and prophets do too.

But when we become aware of the horizons that encircle us, it is an invitation to humility and awe, and it opens us to infinite new ways of interacting with the world.

By bracketing off our anticipation of who we are, or our desire of who we want to be, we sometimes see how we fall short of our image of ourselves. I pride myself on understanding and patience, yet catch myself being short with my teenager or self-righteous with my wife. I know the backstory, my purported justifications, even if they don't. Without my even noticing, I affix an unconscious footnote my self-image and keep it intact.[6]

But when we do pay attention and notice these moments of "defensible hypocrisy", they can serve as a corrective lens with which to see others more clearly. We may never know "why", the reasons that others fall short of the rugged expression of their espoused values. But they too have reasons, explanations and human justifications. Hypocrisy is not an astringent with which to burn others (or ourselves). Rather, it is the salve that clears the gum from our eyes. It allows us to recognize the incompleteness, imperfection and beauty of being human.

All of us are all just trying to figure things out and deserve a pass when we don't get it quite right.

Stripping down the nature of experience also opens us to awe. Awe is one of the world's great collateral promises to us. The universe does not care whether we dawdle at the shopping center or are enraptured by all the possible worlds beyond the horizon. That we evolve toward awe says nothing about *why* the sunrise over the water is so beautiful.

But once we become consciously aware of the infinite worlds that exist just beyond our known horizons, we suddenly become smaller. Rather than diminishing us, a realization of what the horizon suggests, folds us into a greater whole. We become aware that we too are part of the miraculous infinite. When we recognize the marvelous beyond the bounds of perception, our own problems, cares and concerns seem manageable. Following the lives of over 800 people for more than seventy years, psychiatrist George Vaillant points out that the hardships and trials that so concerned us in our youth and at middle age seem small and relatively unimportant against the backdrop of our lives.[7] Yes, we must attend to them in the moment. But like a child weeping with a skinned knee, when we are pulled in close to our mother and held, we know everything is going to be alright. So horizons are temporal too.

These are only a few earnest responses to life. Just as the possibilities beyond the horizon are endless, so too are our potential ways of interacting with the world. The challenge is to embrace the sweet density and obscurity of living, recognize the meaning in the rawness of this human experience, and acknowledge that we may never make sense of it, catch up or understand.

Maybe I am biased by hope. What I do know is there are multiple, credible interpretations of the world. Life is a game, a story, a tragedy, a comedy, a mission, an art, an adventure, a disease, desire, nirvana, selflessness, honor, learning, suffering, an investment, and relationships. At times, life simply is. Whether you believe we only get one shot, or that *how* we live makes a difference in the afterlife or future lives, what you decide now matters. If we must play the game, we might as well play it beautifully, see what we can learn, try to make things better and easier for one another and enjoy the ride as much as we can.[8]

The Great White

The sky. The sea. It could not have been any more clear. My wife and daughters were at the beach enjoying cups of ice cream and sun and strolling out on the wharf. My youngest looked over the rail, and bursting with joy, shouted, "How cool! A shark!" Her excitement was absolute and unrestrained.

My older daughter turned and glanced to where the creature was swimming below. "Oh, a shark," she said. It was a statement of fact. No judgment. Nothing extra. Just neutral and true.

My wife, hearing what the girls had said, looked to the surf and immediately began to scream. "A shark! A shark! Everyone out of the water!"

There was just one shark. But three distinct, credible reactions. Each one appropriate.

We have heard it so often it has become cliché. Our thoughts about things, really are different than the things themselves. The facts about the world, the sharks that are in it, the facts of our lives, are so tied up with our assumptions and fears, our wishes and perceptions. If we recognize this, if we learn to sort the "activating event" from the "belief",[9] then when life happens, we really can decide whether to celebrate or scream.

Of course, we know this, even if we can't always bring it from our head into practice. It is a Stoic truth told from Citium to Athens, and from Rhodes to Rome. It remains a central tenet of cognitive behavioral therapy. But when you are in the middle of it all, when an impetuous boss barks his unreasonable demands, or your teenage daughter rolls her eyes, it is hard to sidestep the anger or frustration. The distinction between "fact" and "thought" is so subtle, so wrapped up in the experience of someone who must live his or her life. I can tell myself that some insecure office clerk with her snide remarks, is not really an ogre after all. That is just my interpretation. Maybe I misunderstood. Maybe this is the only place on the entire planet that she feels that she has autonomy and competence and control.

But this reassessment doesn't stop me from having to live within the dispersive plain of her wrath. It does not shield me from her patronizing disdain.

When we first set about trying to divine the differences between our "thoughts" and the basic "facts", it feels clunky. It is awkward and artificial. Something has gone wrong, or someone is insulting or complaining, and I must sit with a worksheet and pen and diagram the differences between what "really" happened and what I think about it? It can be exhausting. It is easier to just explode than to have to constantly bracket off our emotions.

Yet when we start paying attention, it becomes easier to distinguish the simple, neutral events of the world, from our beliefs or assumptions about those events. It becomes a more natural. We start to notice how our thoughts can get in the way of our effectiveness and joy. And while the beast in the next cube may continue her rant, I am in a better spot from which to respond. It allows me to maintain my center and I can more actively choose how I want to be, and offer a more creative and effective response.

Bad Breath

After the conference had ended and the speakers were stepping off the stage and loosening their ties, a man came forward, bursting with necessity. So much had been said, so much was not said, and he wanted me to understand. He needed someone to understand.

His was one of those cultures in which strong men stood belly-to-belly with other men and kissed them squarely upon the lips. Friends. Business partners. (If only I were so free.) And so, with the urgency of a prophet come up out of the desert, he pressed his soul to mine and plead his case as if we were lovers. My people are a people accustomed to distance. Polite boundaries insured the formality and decorum demanded among strangers.

I moved away with his every urgent step forward, until finally, my back was pressed to the stage. On his breath I could taste the entire history of his race. Garlic and cumin. The soured chickpeas. This man whom I had never seen before tonight carried with him the very stench of the *First Man*, older than Isaiah, as he filled my nostrils and sinuses with transcendence and presence. After all, this odor was a shared birthright. It enveloped me and took root in my chest. It soaked the very spot of my brain[10] where we feel maternal touch and the warmth

23

of bodies; that region that timed every glandular release and paced the circadian rhythm.

How does one respond to the desperation of man? I knew I would never be able to answer his questions. "The fertile crescent is now a desert but at least its people are still warring." And then there were those questions he never did ask, he never would ask, because our most essential longings are untranslatable. They are too sincere. Too human.

This is where the beauty is found. It has little to do with health or youth or symmetry. Beauty is there around the campfire with the village elders and their stories, but it is not the linear narrative. Beauty is rarely found in anyone's first draft of "Truth."

It is that stench of armpits of strangers at every stop sign and cross street.[11] It is a teenage girl, steadying her grandfather at forearm and elbow, as he learns there is honor and joy in depending upon others. Beauty is the novitiate priest come back from his first confession, his ears so filled with sins that the acceptance and forgiveness may finally begin. It is the rib-thin stray, who in a pause between scratching, bows his head, and laps sunrise from the puddles.

Lift up your eyes to the human dignity. Seek from every moment, the humor, the tenderness, the honesty that is there in the way we live our lives, regardless of what the "facts" say. That is where beauty resides. Every fact we have expressed, every thought we have ever had - be they the distant musings for a better world or the intimate hesitancies softly shared - were simply ideas. The ideas never understood that their purpose was to inform beauty.

24

And so often in this life we must live with facts that we'd never wish for. The buildings in which we'd sought shelter year after year inevitably fall into disrepair. They decay and are overcome by flowering weeds. Beauty is not that which stretches out before our eyes. It is what lies behind and beneath and above all the crass and mundane facts. It never will be the cancer that soaked your neighbor to the bone. But it is the way in which she has learned to adapt and to love and to sometimes even accept. It is not the smoke stack adding gray to an already gray cityscape. But it is the people coming to and from that factory every day after day because they understand what is required and so go about their living. Every pretty thing will fade and wrinkle. But the honor that comes with the age spots and entropy, with having outlasted the simply-pretty, is the subtle, more lasting and sustainable truth called beauty. Walking around the lake each morning, everywhere, invisible fish kiss the roof of their world.

I turned again to this strange cousin and looked into his eyes, grown wide. Man-to-man, I stepped forward, and with droplets of spit kissing face, I inhaled what was our common breath.

Changing the Narrative

The stories we tell ourselves matter. They make a difference in how we think about who we are and the way we structure our lives. They affect the paths we blaze and those we follow. Our stories inform every sigh and every tear, keep us afloat, and connect us to the ones we love.

But so often, these stories that are so fundamental to who we are, are based upon just *some* of the facts from our complex and beautiful lives. We are our stories, no doubt. But we are so much more too.

I remember the day my parents came and told me I would be held back in the first grade. We had recently moved. My sister had just been born. There were many other distractions for an otherwise distractible young boy.

It was summertime and I wanted to play. I didn't give the matter any other thought. But when school began again the following year, and all the children went out for recess, I saw my friends on top of the hill. That is where the second graders played. Looking up, I deduced they must be smarter than me.

My parents had handled the matter with elegance and grace. Throughout my life, they could not have given me more love or support. With patience and care they explained why they and the teachers decided I should repeat first grade. I *did* need an extra year. Not everyone matures in the same way or at the same time. But thereafter, anytime anything was hard - first grade, middle school, when I was still getting "Ds" in senior high - it all made sense. "*It was difficult,*" I thought, "*because I was not as smart as the other kids.*"[12]

When I was accepted into the honors program at my college, I thought I had fooled them. My advisor gave a stiff critique of my thesis (as advisors do) and I felt I had finally been "found out". I dropped out of that program. Then there was law school. Then there was the big firm where only the top students from the top schools would go. Every time anything was difficult, it was all the proof I needed that I did not belong.

But the whole time, there were other truths too. In third grade, Mrs. Kujala selected my poem from among all of those in the class to hang on the wall. Or there was that time Mr. Modispaugh encouraged me to sign up for honors biology. There were other teachers too. There were the things my parents pointed out. These other facts were there the whole time and could have told a different story, that I didn't hear.

I had never heard of growth mindset.[13] I thought "intelligence" was something fixed, not a quality that could be developed or expanded. I never sensed what the philosophers and physicists knew: No matter how many facts we have, there will be many theories that explain them. Our very lives are bundles of hypotheses.[14] At six-years

28

old, I took the evidence collected by me and made a cognitive commitment[15] that affected and governed my life for years. I never knew that the fact that things were difficult or hard could mean many things. I only let it feed my self-doubt.[16] Maybe things were difficult for the other kids too? Maybe some things that I found easy, were hard for others. Maybe the key to "intelligence" or "success" or getting along with your teenager is in going to the limits and rough patches of your world and playing within that space; rejoicing when we stumble and noticing all the possible futures it reveals.

How often do we do that in our lives? We hold fast to facts that are absolutely true: Sometimes, joyful; sometimes, tragic. We look at how we have been neglected or abused or taken advantage of, and weave these truths into a story that is somehow **less** than true. We become nothing but *that* narrative.[17]

Along the way, you may have been broken or violated. Honor that. But you are more than that too. Often the stories we tell ignore how brave we've been or how resourceful, how funny or how wise. Too often our stories neglect the healing and growth that is possible and that we continue to be alive. We let very real travesties go on and traumatize and cripple, long after their shadow has passed. We are more than the stories we tell.[18]

Keep the narratives you've written for their limited truths. But learn also to let go. We are always capable of the best futures we can imagine.

I am not sure what sparked the change in me: whether it was something someone said, or if I became aware of other truths that were there the whole time. What I do know is that the bad things in life demand our attention. They are "stronger" than the good.[19] We argue with someone we love and say something we regret, and it takes five positive acts to undo every one negative.[20] So we absolutely must keep putting the good stuff out there. We must treat people better than they are, because only then, in Goethe's words, can they become what they are capable of becoming.[21]

Think back to a time when someone did something - offered you a kindness, or treated you in some manner - that changed you. Maybe it caused you to go into a different career. Maybe, for the first time, you saw a strength or talent you never knew you had. But somehow, what they said or did fundamentally changed the way you saw yourself. These "trigger moments" might be positive, or they could be hurtful too. Either way, we never know who is going to say that thing that matters, or when. It could be a teacher or a neighbor. Most likely, when that person was saying whatever it was that altered the arc of your life, they had no idea.

When talking with a group about these trigger moments, a teacher rose and spoke. He had been the director of a middle school choir. Voices cracking, masculinity straining to take root, none of the early-pubescent boys wanted to join. He would approach them individually, talk to them and try to convince them to sing.

The teacher told us that one boy he recruited stayed in touch long after he left the school. He went to senior high and college, and eventually invited his favorite teacher to his wedding. At the reception, the young groom pulled his choirmaster aside. *"I don't know if you knew,"* he said, *"but all those years ago, when you asked me to join the choir, things were difficult. I was having a hard time,"* he said. *"I had been thinking about taking my own life."*

There was a pause.

"And yet when you reached out, and showed an interest in me and let me know that I mattered in some way, that made all the difference."[22] No one in the room exhaled.

The teacher continued, *"I wish I knew what I had said."* He told us. *"I was just trying to get boys to join the choir."*

We never know when we are going to affect someone in big and meaningful ways - for the better, or for the worse. We never know when we are going to do something or say some word that changes another person's narrative so that they see wonderful new truths about their lives. And precisely because the bad is so much stronger than the infinite goodness' of our every day, we must keep putting the good stuff out there, again and again and again.

Hold one another's eyes a little bit longer. Ask questions and listen for the things people don't know how to say. Point to all the beautiful, wonderful and wonderous things in their lives and leave them better than you found them. We are all more than the stories we tell. You have the infinite power to make others see just how miraculous and beautiful they can be.

Part II. Being Towards Others

Refuge in Love

Sometimes the things of life can shatter your world. Not just the traumas we know to expect: The death of a loved one, or how with the passage of time, we watch our own bodies decay. Even if we have banished these inevitable facts of our lives to the farthest edges of possibility, somewhere beneath awareness we know that one day they will occur. As hard and as real as they are, they were written into the script before we began. Human beings are evolved for adaptation. With time, clinging to what centers us, and a little holding of hands, we endure, we can even thrive.

But what happens when the hardship, the trauma, cuts directly at that which centers us? When the unthinkable strikes those beliefs that were our foundations? What about when the things we relied upon in structuring and ordering our lives can no longer be trusted? How are we to respond when we lived our lives as if the world were good and safe and beautiful, and someone or something ripped that from us along with our hearts?

Of course, I am not six years old. I know bad things happen and that sometimes people take advantage of the innocent, vulnerable or trusting. Injustice has been with us longer than Christ. I am not talking about a loss of innocence that, to a certain degree, is part of normal maturation. Rather, what happens when another being betrays our trust in such an intimate way that there is nothing left of what we believed about the world?

Giving up, or giving in to despair, is easy and natural. But doing so never can protect or heal. In the face of hardship, injustice or the coldest of traumas, the only answer is love. When everything is out of control, the only thing we can do is give ourselves over to a universe we cannot control and hold even tighter to kindness. Even if the pain we feel was caused by people acting cruelly to one another, the only response that can save us, *is caring even more deeply.*

As soon as we stop caring and stop being surprised at the world's unjust indiscretions, we lose that which is the most human thing about us. Anger burns everyone. Especially the one who holds it. By taking refuge in love, we are healed again, purified, and the ground is prepared for new growth.

I know it sounds naïve or trite to say that in the face of hardship or trauma, the only answer is love. However whether in the workplace, our personal lives, or even the tight spots in life, both research and experience prove this to be true.

As a five or six-year-old child, I used to go with my parents to visit an elderly relative. Alcohol, anger, and hardship had ravaged her for years. I don't tell this story to shame or blame in any way. We don't get to choose the angels or demons that take up residence in our lives. We wrestle with the torments as best as we can, but sometimes we are overwhelmed.

My parents would send me to the playground or to the next room to watch reruns in black-and-white as they helped her with her taxes, her medical issues, and other troubles. Over the static of the TV, I remember her screaming at them, and my father gently handing her groceries or money to help with her bills. I don't know what was said. I don't know what my parents wrestled with privately or together back at home. But I did see that under duress, they fed her kindness. All those years ago I was too young and tender to notice, but those moments of respect and care and calm were my first lessons in subtlety.

Conflict is inevitable. The weak will be exploited. You will be hurt by your friends and loved ones. Coworkers and strangers will insult and belittle you. People can be remarkably cruel. But none of this means that violence is inevitable; not physical violence, not emotional violence, not verbal violence, and not even an anger held in our hearts. There is one response that is both effective and allows us to maintain our sense of integrity, humanity and respect: love.

You are cut off in traffic. A coworker sends you a snippy email. Your teenager rolls her eyes at you. You are passed over for a promotion. The homeowner's association sends you a certified letter complaining that you left your garbage at the curb too long. At the church fish fry, a neighbor spreads gossip about a friend. When the other responds to us with a poke in the eye, it is easy to feel hurt, frustrated, and angry.

Sometimes we try to persuade with reason. Sometimes, we want to hit back. When a cyberbully lobs condescending or incendiary bombs at us in public, it feels good to beat them over the head with their own stupidity or triteness. A violent repartee to violence feels justified. In our counter attack, we feel vindicated.

But hours later, back at home again, reliving the experience with friend or spouse, our heart is still racing and our blood pressure, still climbing. So often, any trace of a positive feeling that accompanied the sense of justification falls away, and we feel a little dirtier, and a little cheaper, that we allowed ourselves to be made worth less.

Further, it is unlikely that the hostile response even worked. After disabusing the bully, does he have a moment of clarity and insight, apologize, and thank you for showing him the error of his ways? Of course not. Maybe he tucked his tail between his legs and briefly stopped his public ranting, at least for now. However, the only thing violence really does is dehumanize the other. While it may have appeared to work in the short term, it does not really *work*.

Violence always hurts someone, somewhere. We know it hurts the recipient. But tragically it also hurts us, and it injures any witnesses to the carnage. How we treat one another spreads outward through networks and effects strangers and loved ones alike.

Happiness, loneliness, altruism, and whether people cheat all spread through networks. [23] If people cooperate, it is more likely that strangers, three degrees removed, will also cooperate. Like an event cone, one act, whether it inserts humanity or hostility, changes and alters seemingly unrelated events.

It is this dynamic that lay behind what Gandhi called *satyagraha* or soul force. The strength of nonviolence is not in weapons or numeric advantage, but in clinging to truth. It is not easy or soft or passive. It does not involve ignoring injustice or wishing it would go away. Rather satyagraha's steadfast commitment to humanity and refusal to inflict harm can take tremendous strength, courage, and stamina. It requires you to stare unblinkingly in the face of hostility for extended periods of time, under extreme conditions, with no guarantee that you will be successful in the immediate situation.

Very often, increasing humanity in the midst of crisis might not feel like it works. Cheaters often get away with it. People who stab us in the back or suck up at work, sometimes get rewarded. However often it does work in the short term. As a lawyer who has negotiated over 10,000 disputes, I have seen this again and again. An invitation to understanding, empathy, or respect, gives the other a backdoor out of their own hostility and a pathway to resolution.

Importantly, as peace scholar Michael Nagler points out, while nonviolence sometimes works in the immediate moment, it always *works* on a larger scale.[24] If we interrupt the violence and insert humanity into inhuman situations, that goodness, kindness, and love will also spread and affect how others deal with one another. We might not be immediately aware of how or why, but when we increase the humility, compassion, understanding, vulnerability, kindness or love, somewhere it will heal and build.

For psychiatrist George Vaillant,[25] we were meant to be bound together. Our brains are wired for social connection: for love, respect, appreciation, acceptance, sympathy, empathy, compassion, and tenderness. These are the things that connect us. These biologically-based, spiritual emotions reach the other at levels that pure reason can never touch. Satyagraha does not change the positions of the parties. It changes their relationship.

When my parents responded to a drunk, despondent and aggravated old woman with compassion and respect, they did not know that this kindness would reach the child quietly listening in the next room, plant seeds in his soul, and continue to grow outward for forty years.

Whether we are seeking peace in middle school or the Middle East, whether the bully is in the lunch room or the board room, in most circumstances, the most effective strategy is the one that increases the amount of humanity between people.[26]

Hugging the Horse's Head

In January 1889, Friedrich Nietzsche went insane. Armed with metaphor, irony and aphorism, the German philosopher carved his influence deep into twentieth century culture, criticism, literature and psychology. Freud, Mann, Yeats, Richard Strauss and countless other artists and thinkers were shaped by the "First Immoralist". In popular culture, Nietzsche was idolized and vilified for his Zarathustra coming down out of his cave in the mountains with an eagle and a staff and declaring that God was dead.

But despite the death of God, despite the nihilism and the altered manuscripts, Nietzsche's writing affirmed life. It was filled with courage. Nietzsche embraced the hardships, boundaries and sickness of the world and called upon each of us to stretch beyond the social constructs of culture and the moral legacy that is our inheritance.

But then on January 3, 1889, everything unraveled. While in an open-air market in Turin, Nietzsche witnessed a merchant flogging a horse. He ran to the animal and yelled for the beating to stop. He threw himself between beast and whip, and hugged the equine's thick neck. This frail and sickly philosopher who gave us the *Übermensch* and slave morality, then collapsed, weeping.

I understand why Nietzsche hugged the horses' head. Life is hard. It is not fair. It is filled with rapturous beautiful moments and it all ends much, much too quickly. When we look around and see so many people who are unnecessarily cruel, or mindless, or oblivious to inequities; when we see our brothers and neighbors exhaling their numbered breaths in ways that add to the pain or take from the sympathy, we see a world that is, in fact, more absurd and nihilistic than anything the philosopher wrote or said or thought. To see these mindless cruelties playout before him was simply too much for the philosopher to bear; especially when the remedy, the antidote - even our purpose for being here - is so very clear.

Nietzsche was a pastor's son. Raised on nagging hypocrisies and half-truths of a faith half-applied, Nietzsche rejected everything. The prophets did too: Jeremiah and Isaiah, Mohammad and Siddhartha. Even Christ. But whether obvious or ironic, the remedy Nietzsche felt was there, at the center, all along. It is that certain truth, absolute but malleable, at the center of every faith tradition. We look up from our desks or push ourselves away from the table and see people treated unfairly at work or on the playground or at the church fish fry. It happens in our very own homes. Yet all any of us need, all every one of us need, is understanding, patience, kindness, and simple human respect. Every one of us is just bumping around trying the best we can. Everyone one of us is dealing with the same raw adaptive imperatives: births, deaths and the sufferings and sicknesses of loved ones. We wake in the morning with a new tumor or must move our bowels in a bag hung under our shirts or we struggle to find answers or reasons for so many human dilemmas that are simply a part of living. No wonder sometimes we ourselves can be unknowingly cruel or thoughtless or rudely blunt. Yet we are all just doing our best. In a world where we all make mistakes, where our motives are misunderstood, the only answer that makes sense is to give ourselves over to kindness, forgiveness, patience and understanding.

Go down to the marketplace. Empty your pockets of fear and self-consciousness. Lay everything you are out bare on a blanket. Exchange what you thought was in your "best interest" for a more humane humility. For one day, the horse's head we will be hugging, will be pointing toward eternity.

Whatever Happened to Conner MacBride?

Thoughts of peer pressure bring a parent's worst fears to mind: sex; drugs; uncategorized acts of stupidity; the fact that our kids cannot be who they are, when they are, the most themselves. When they get home at night, there is no escape from the prancing of peers on Instagram and Vine, teasing over Twitter, or the torment on Facebook. And even we, in our adult dignity, are not immune. There are the ladies in the garden club with their hats; the bosses whose only ethic is a personal P&L; and gossip at the neighborhood bake sale. How many times have we watched as someone was treated unfairly at work, and yet we could not intervene?

There is another kind of peer pressure too.

One night, sometime back in high school when we were still young and indestructible, we were out drinking too much with friends and the friends-of-friends. These were not the "good" kids. They were the ones who smoked between class, if they went to class at all. They got into fights and got suspended. They painted curses on the walls. Several of the boys had used the heaviest drugs, the ones we were taught to fear. Yes, I drank, and I was too young. But I never was tempted by or desired those other drugs.

But on this night of whisky, beer and diminished judgment, someone pulled out psychedelic mushrooms and it caused me to pause. They seemed more interesting. They seemed more aligned with my seventeen-year-old poetic and philosophic nature. So as the plastic bag was passed from person-to-person sitting in a circle on the floor, my curiosity and interest grew.

To my right sat Conner MacBride. We were friendly, no doubt, but he was not among my closest friends. He consumed the heaviest drugs in the largest portions. There were rumors about his home. Rumors that no one wanted to imagine true. Sometime much later, he would be kicked out of school and sent away.

The mushrooms were passed from hand-to-hand, from stranger-to-friend and to Conner MacBride. Then, suddenly, they leapt past me in a toss. Conner MacBride, that lotus-eater, the child that all of the parents feared, looked me straight in the eyes, raised the whisky bottle level with our gaze, and told me with great sobriety that if he ever heard I was doing drugs, he would smash the bottle over my head. "You are the only one in this room that has a chance," he said, "you are worth more than this."

Where did you go, Conner MacBride? What happened to you, and to all the people in our lives, those somewhere between friend and stranger, who watch over us from the margins and shadows like angels who have fallen and know how much it hurts?

Our friends will be there for us time and time again, year after-year, but sometimes they too will let us down. Sometimes our dearest friends are the ones who administer the pressure we fear. They are after all, just as flawed and tempted and confused as any of us. Honor this truth. Forgive them. Keep them in your hearts. But sometimes what we need are our tarnished peers. Sometimes the pressure from those around us is not to be feared. Tender moments are often shared in the harshest of ways and in the darkest of places.

I don't know now if I would have tasted the mushrooms on that night. Or if I had, whether the arc of my life would have shifted. But looking in the dilated unblinking eyes of someone no one trusted, I learned that trust was the only thing that mattered. That the day-in, day-out decency we offer one another, that our humanity demands we offer, sometimes makes a difference without us ever knowing. That if we honor ourselves by honoring others, that others will be there in dark rooms giving back, so brutally, so beautifully.

Absence and Return

Community can take many forms. We can find one another in many places. For several years, I had been loosely involved with an online Buddhist *Sangha*. After a while, I began to get more active and made some commitments to the group. I was going to meditate more. I would be more mindful in my eating. One night each week, I would volunteer in the community. I even started to sew a robe.

However, as the days continued to turn and filled with their deadlines and demands, my good intentions began to slip. First for a day. Then two or three. Before I realized it, I had forgotten my commitments and returned to the mindless, thoughtless routine.

There is a certain comfort in routine. It is safe and easy. Predicable and familiar. However, it brings a sort of emptiness too. After a while, I longed for the peace and care offered by the community. I started to meditate. I paid attention to the textures, smells and source of my food.

I wanted to return to the site but was embarrassed. How would I explain my absence? Not only did I fail to keep my commitments, but I no longer remembered exactly what they were. I decided that at first,

I would just visit the site and read the latest threads, but like a voyeur, not announce my presence.

The first post I saw was of one of the members saying goodbye.

I had read and responded to her comments for years. However, in the months I was gone, she had received a diagnosis and entered hospice. Now, she could no longer manage the computer and was gracefully closing things.

All the while I had been worried about me: How I would look; What of the promises I had made, and of my stumbles?

How often do we do this in life? The neighbor brimming with health and hope has a miscarriage. Or she softly expresses concern that her father has begun forgetting things. Or, there is that couple you have known for years who just announced their divorce, and a cousin you love but lost touch with who discovered a spot on his lungs.

We express condolences, or at least intend to, but are uncomfortable and don't know what to say. And then we return to the habits and routines and mundane stresses that provide a comfortable predictability in our lives.

What's more, even though we don't believe it and would strongly disavow the thought, it is easy to feel that our lives are somehow more important, more relevant. Looking outward through my eyes it seems my life is special and different, as if it were my hopes and fears that dotted the night sky.[27] The neighbor's miscarriage or cancer or concern does not feel as real as if it were mine. And as much as I do care, I cannot allow myself to feel every pain and fear and concern of loved ones and strangers as deeply as if they were my own.

But life, even our own, is not about us. We are part of something bigger; a more intricate fabric. It is softer. It stretches beyond where we are now. The way we encounter one another – how we listen, how we respond, whether we touch – matters. Soften yourself. Set aside those important things that keep you so distracted. And just hold one another with your gaze, in your heart, and take care of the matters that are bigger than all of us.

The Sacred Thread

The little space within the heart is as great as the vast universe.[28] When I arrived for my friend's wedding in India, I was the first of our group. The bride invited me to a family ceremony at her home. All the uncles and icons were there. A Hindu priestess came and lit a fire in the sitting room. She boiled ayurvedic herbs in copper pots and fed the deity milk mixed with floral oils, Ghee, banyan chips and turmeric root. Her Sanskrit prayers for the couple rose with the fragrant smoke.

At the end of the ceremony, the officiant tied a sacred red thread around my wrist. I was told to never take it off. Once it fell by its own natural causes, I was to place it under a tree where the purification, dedication and protection from evil sown by the prayers would take root and spread.

A sacred red thread appears in many forms in Hinduism. The love between siblings is marked by tying a holy thread around the wrist. Serving as a bond of protection, this thread pulsates with sisterly love and sublime sentiments and serves as a mark that the strong must protect the weak. This protective tether stretches beyond the bonds of biology or blood. When tied to close friends and neighbors, the thread demands harmony in social life, and calls upon everyone to co-exist as brothers and sisters.

Throughout Indian history the exchange of a thin cotton, wool or silk thread tied kingdoms together and sealed political alliances. In one recount of the Battle of the Hydaspes River, it is said that the King Porus refrained from striking Alexander the Great, because Alexander's wife had tied a sacred thread to Porus' hand, urging him not to hurt her husband.

A scarlet or red thread runs through many other cultures too.

The red string of fate or the thread of destiny appears in both Chinese and Japanese legends where the gods tie an invisible scarlet string around the ankles of those that are destined to meet or care for one another. In another myth, two people connected by the red thread are destined to be lovers, regardless of time, place or circumstance. The cord may stretch or tangle across the years, but it will never break.

In traditional Tibetan Buddhist ceremonies, the tying on of holy cotton threads restores the natural order of things and brings people closer together. The red thread is specifically associated with bravery.

And this sacred tie is not limited to East Asia.

In Greek mythology, Theseus rescued himself from the labyrinth of the Minotaur by following a red thread that was given to him by Ariadne. Nikos Kazantzakis, in making myths modern again, points to the scarlet thread that runs through and connects all people, friends and strangers, regardless of culture.[29] It is our common humanity.

In Judaism, wearing a thin red string on the left wrist is thought to ward off misfortune brought by the "evil eye". Rahab tied a scarlet rope to two scouts, so they could enter Jericho unseen. Jacob's wife Rachel, the mother of Joseph and Benjamin, wrapped a red thread around her son's wrist to protect him from evil. Still today, we tie a long red string around her burial stone. This sacred symbol recalls Rachel's selflessness, reminding us to emulate her modest ways of consideration and compassion for others, while giving charity to the poor and needy. More than just protection from evil or harm, the crimson thread is an internal reflection that inspires good deeds and kindness.

When deeply rooted, rituals sustain us and strengthen our hearts as we navigate the various hardships of life. They induce connection, open up channels of communication, and give us an opportunity to rediscover that which is the most human within us. What is common to these myths and rituals is a sense of caring and connection between people. Whether it be love or an obligation to protect, or a call to increase our acts of kindness, there is a thread of humanity that runs through all of us, unrestrained by culture or class, race or religion.

One need not be a priest or mystic or saint to see this link between all of us. You need only set aside self-interest and soften your hearts, and a magical scarlet web will fill the visual plane: stretching between strangers in airports; between students in middle school lunchrooms; between joggers picking up newspapers for old women in pink bath robes. Once we see this thread extending from our own hearts, we cannot help but feel the pulse of compassion that beats within all of us.

After about a year, the thread tied to my wrist had long since faded, and fell off when we were working in an orphanage in Guatemala. I placed the muted talisman under a flowering carnation tree in the courtyard so its prayers for protection, goodness and connection would be shared with the children, and would spread and grow.

Throwing Bullets in the Fire

When we first moved to the place I would come to call home, a boy, five years my senior, knocked on the door to meet his new playmate. He introduced himself, spelt his last name, and every weekend and summer we played. Sometimes in the woods pretending we were soldiers or Indians or runaways, off to find our fortunes. Sometimes down at creek, building dams or pursuing elusive crawfish we would never admit we were too scared to catch. One Christmas day when we were taking turns with his older brother's toy plane, it sputtered and fell and broke. David was the one who was blamed and beaten, and I learned something about accidents and injustice.

And then there was the time when he took some of the bullets from his father's gun and we went out behind the school. I must have been six. We gathered rocks from the playground and laid them in a ring. Then we filled the circle with sticks and twigs and leaves. A little gas and a single match was all we needed to bring the pile to flame. As the fire grew hungrier and more demanding, David reached in his pocket and fed our creation a handful of the stolen shells and we ran for shelter.

We waited. And we waited. And we waited with all of the patience and wild blood of innocent young boys. When nothing happened, we walked out into the open just before the explosions began, just before something unseen struck the tree inches from where we stood.

I don't know how many mistakes I've made in life or how many near misses there have been. Like when I touched the socket in the dark, or thought I could balance on the ladder while carrying a saw, or when I looked up from the phone just in time to slam on the brakes. There have been innumerous times I acted rudely or without thinking, yet was lucky enough to walk away as the shrapnel harmlessly sprayed a nearby tree.

Yet we pick up the paper every day and know that sometimes jagged scraps do strike an eye, lodge in the heart or spray the strangers who did nothing wrong. Cheaply made toy planes falter and fall. Someone pulls out in front of us while we are switching songs on the radio. We look at the mindless and senseless things that kids and grown-ups do and it is easy to blame. *How can they be so stupid, so shortsighted? Didn't they think about it for a moment?* But as long as there is no ricochet or crash, we are allowed to forget that we too are irresponsible and thoughtless. Every one of us is negligent. But to be negligent and unlucky? That is a crime no one can ever shake off.

Had the bullet that day exploded and lodged in the chest of my friend, I would have been the one toward whom the neighbors would point. I would be one of the bad kids, poorly raised or unthinking.

Stupid and reckless or irresponsible. I would have been the one to carry those jagged shards in my heart forever.

Luck, that blind mistress and kin to Fate, can be kind. She can be horribly cruel. We can look on our own misfortunes or windfalls or those of others, and we too can be kind or cruel. But we can be more than that. We must be more than that.

The world is neither fair nor reasonable nor within our control. Even the best laid plans fail. Even with the most fully thought out actions, there is no escape. Whether it is misuse or overuse or neglect, the things of our lives fall apart. And yet we have at our finger tips so many more tools than any fickle goddess could dream. Kindness, yes. But also, humility, forgiveness, understanding, patience. So much patience. And the ability to roll up our sleeves and reach out a hand and help one another. And the fortitude to push aside judgments as useless as blame, and pick up the pieces, and put them back again.

Part III. Overcoming and Acceptance

Lost at Sea

No one knew when or where John Aldridge had fallen off his lobster boat.[30] It was some time the middle of the night. His boat had traveled for hours and another twenty miles before anyone discovered he was missing. Aldridge was lost in a swath of ocean the size of Rhode Island.

Author and reporter Paul Tough[31] describes what Aldridge did to survive the 72-degree, shark-thick water for twelve hours with the knowledge that rescue was a near impossibility. At some point in our lives, everyone of us will be lost, adrift at sea. Maybe we will be navigating a difficulty at work, or dealing with a loved one's illness. Maybe we will be fighting to keep our heads above water when drowning in debt. The essential lesson of survival and success in the face of any hardship is learning to remain positive and recognizing the things that keep us afloat.

Many people confuse the relationship between optimism and "reality". We tend to believe that as serious thinkers, businesspeople or lawyers, we have to reside in the folds of cynicism and skepticism. However, a pessimist can be just as wrong and unrealistic as an optimist, and with deadly consequences. Even self-claimed "realists" slam the door on the opportunities, possibilities and facts that are right before them. Realistically, John Aldridge should have died.

In its survival training, the US Air Force teaches the *Rule of Three*. [32] You cannot live more than three weeks without food, three days without water or three minutes without air. Equally important, you cannot survive more than three seconds without spirit or hope. When we abandon hope, as is inscribed on the gates of hell, we lose our ability both to recognize what we can control, and to take appropriate action. Hope is not ignoring the facts of a given situation or a wishing for a miracle. It is not a promise that you will survive being lost at sea, turn around a failing product line or learn to trust again after a loved one betrays you. Hope is goal-directed thinking.[33] It requires a sense of efficacy:[34] a recognition of what you can control. If we allow ourselves to get lost in the vastness of the problem - being adrift at night in the midst of the sea, losing your job or being diagnosed with cancer - it can crush our spirit. It can blind us to the things right before our eyes that can aid in our survival or promote our growth, thriving and meaning.

Rather than focus on a reality as deep as the ocean, Aldridge just tried to stay afloat until morning. When daylight came, he set his next goal: Find a buoy. Go as far as you can see, and then you will be able to see further.

Rather than discard his boots as deadweight as he had been taught, Aldridge found that they could help him float and delay fatigue. You may already have the resources you need at your feet to help you shoulder your burden. You will only notice them if you remain hopeful, positive and open.

And when after nine hours in the water, a boat passed within quarter mile on its way to the horizon, Aldridge did not allow his spirit to sink. He bound two buoys together so he could rest his sunburnt, exhausted body. Despite everything we have longed for, striven toward, or based our lives upon, there is so much that we cannot control. From time-to-time, life unexpectedly reaches out and bludgeons us. But if we accept these soul-shattering disappointments as the entirety of our fate, we will fail to lash together those things that keep us afloat. In addition to helping us find a pathway to our desired goals, hope keeps us going. It involves "agency" thinking.[35] It provides the energy, motivation and fuel to keep us moving. Without hope, Aldridge would have likely given up, and not taken the steps that kept him alive.

Of course, many people who remain positive drown in the sea, persist too long at failing businesses, or have their faith betrayed and hearts broken. Every survivor story, every success story, is also a story of luck. Just as there are those who survive and others who would have died no matter what they did, there are a percentage of people whose death could have been avoided; people who remained buckled in their seats as the plane burned around them.

Regardless of what hard, brutal facts life presents, maintain your calm. Keep looking for what you can control. Pay attention to how your routines and everyday objects might yield new tools or insights. Look for the helpers that are all around you all the time. And never let go of the hope that will keep you going.

It Is Not the Mountain We Conquer

I t is inevitable.[36] From time to time, when least expected, *Life* will reach out and find you. You could be *eating or opening a window or just walking dully along*[37] and you feel the familiar tap of a hand stretching out as it hangs its heavy burdens around your neck. It is as if every now and then *Life*, graceless and unrefined, demands of us an answer. *"How are we to make sense of it all?"* Over time, the hopes and dreams that once shimmered on our miraculous horizons have been dulled by drudgery and disappointments, false starts, obligations and pain. We are left wondering who we are, what we've become and where we are going.

Yet we continue on and discover we are stronger than we believed. With tenacity and persistence, patience and love, and maybe a few tears, we push aside the charmless bangles *Life* brings and we persist. In our better moments of unrestrained hope, we may even stay up late, stand strong in the sadness or self-doubt, and make those deliberate choices about how we want to live our lives. Whether with clear heads or foolishness, we go and seek struggles in which to cloak ourselves. Despite conditions. Despite the obligations and limited time.

Despite the pockmarks in our less-than-perfect lives, sometimes it is we who stand up and say "*Yes, this is how I am going to live my life.*"

Maybe there just comes a time when after going to a job every day, fixing the broken things and trimming the hedges, we wake to an alarm to do it all again and recognize we need something. So almost fifty and too long behind a desk, I entered a 100 mile backwoods mountain bike race. Thirteen thousand feet of climbing. Seven mountain peaks. Having reached the age of hernias and hemorrhoids, I went to the mountains to press against the impossible and irascible, to court pain and fatigue and look in my heart to try to distinguish between prudence and truth.

As the sun rose over the mountainscape that summer morning, I tightened my helmet and clipped my feet firmly into the pedals. Mourning doves cooed to cows in the rolling pasture land and my life began. It only took a few miles into the first climb, my first adulthood, to discover you cannot simulate mountains when you live near the sea.

I pressed. I pushed. I powered up slopes longer and steeper than I imagined, and after cresting the first of seven peaks, my exhilaration was higher than the conquered mountain beneath my feet.

Up above the ridgeline where the sky was the shape and hue of heaven, the descent was long and fast and it fooled me with its joy. As the afternoon turned into night, there were longer climbs, steeper, and with rockier descents. Every dream and doubt and demon of a lifetime were there to introduce me to what it means to be alive.

As you climb whatever mountains you've dreamed, as you fight to forge the legacies you'll leave, you will slog through boredom, and your mind and body will scream songs of doubt and pain and demand that you stop. Whatever called you to the mountain, whatever you are chasing or running from, will not be enough. The mountain will look you in the eye again and again as if it cared, and demand that you renew your vows with a clarity that is honest and raw and never simple.

Maybe you had something to prove. Maybe it was a last gasp to hold on to the past and glory and youth for just one more year. That may have been enough to get you to the line. But the long days and painful nights, the hours of tedium, demand something more. At times it will be your anger or spite that drive you. Every time you flirted with a dream or dared those first tentative steps, there were those who feigned support but only siphoned your energies. Empty and depleted, the sustenance you were promised was nothing more than an anemic broth in a slotted spoon. Or the anger may be at those who watched your labors, sensed a lash of doubt in your eye, and declared as true the things you most feared: *You are not good enough; You will never do it; No one cares.*

I am not above the human habitus for hurt and anger. But as if both spark and kindling, the outrage and offense transmute to flame and fuel me onward. No mountain can match that pain.

But fires burn out leaving nothing. So when *Life* continues its demands, something more is required. Something deeper, richer, like love. There were so many back at home who believed in you, who entrusted you with their faith: Lovers and family; Your closest friends; Those who have slipped from your every day. Your life is filled with people who want your dream for you, who need what you have to offer.

It is the people in your present and those from your past who believe that you are good and worthy and have something meaningful to give. One part Faust, another Sisyphus, there were so many nights when you were pushing and fighting and raging against an indifferent universe as your children were in bed and your wife was sleeping. Or every Sunday after Saturday after the weekend before when you left your friends behind, when you turned from the things you love, and refused what is good for you and brings you joy, knowing full well they were the direct paths to happiness, because you had something more to give. To push over mountaintops, to write a book or leave something lasting behind, never had anything to do with you. It is about honoring those who honored you. It is about honoring those who believed there was something in life that was good and gentle and worth fighting for. Conquering mountains is an act of love.

Hour after straining-hour of rutted switchbacks and gnarled roots. The sandy ascents. Something more is still needed to find traction amid rocks as jagged as our own uncertain hesitancies.

To empty oneself. To gasp at air as if it were our first or our last breath. Something holy is there waiting for us. We glimpse God when we look beyond our self-doubt. We touch God when we push through what we feared was a void, only to discover awe.

No one thing keeps us pressing over mountain tops. It is all of these, and other reasons unspoken.[38] Your legs cramp in the middle of a climb. The boss or border guard tells you "no". The lover to whom you've tethered your hopes and dreams and memories walks out. Nothing in life asks any more of us than when we are clinging to a dream. It is when we are fully engaged that we feel the most alive. It is the intimate intensity that reminds us that we are not just lingering on our way to death.

Hunched against a tree. Gasping for breath. You vomit and get to choose. Do you listen to the lies your head will tell you? *I am underprepared. I will never make it. I was foolish to ever leave the cubicle and chase a dream.* Or do you recognize the simple truths of the body? Not every pain is a signal to stop. Not every throb or stab gets worse if we persist. Maybe I just didn't get my nutrition right. So the body recalibrates, the stomach clears itself, and I am ready to go on.

All the joys and all the doubts were still there. The rocky inclines and muscle cramps. The loose stones and fatigue. The drop-offs and spasms. After the longest climb asked me every question all over again, I dialed down a mountain of crumbling stone. All terror and beautiful ecstasy. It was then during the afterglow, once the rocks were cleared, that I crashed. A year later, feeling calcium deposits in my leg, the emergency room doctor would say I fractured my knee cap that day. But more grit than sense, more dedication than skill, I continued to ride to the shadow of an even greater mountain. The aides in the support station would say it was the hardest, the most dangerous section, on the course.

I wanted this to be a story about glory, about honor. How overweight and over the hill I overcame a swollen knee and the pain of Achilles to conquer the mountains. But sometimes glory is not what is printed in the papers. Sometimes it is soft-spoken and beneath notice. You'll find it standing somewhere other than on the top step wearing a myrtle wreath. Glory can be the simple act of walking up to the line, whether stoic or with tears, staring in the face of your greatest fears. We seek challenges the size and shape of our own doubts because who we "are" is not something pure and refined at the center of our being.[39] Nor are we those heart-held aspirations we've yet to achieve. We are hybrid creatures, both mud and dreams. There is no contradiction between gritty determination and appropriate disengagement. It is when we press the limits of who we are that we discover ourselves as honest and alive. It is when we look through our tears into the unblinking stare of our doubts and our fears that we uncover our greatest beauty, strength and majesty. The essence of who we are resides in the margins of our lives. It is in these border lands where we take the first great taste of salty freedom.

I did not finish the race on that summer day. It is a race I am still running. That afternoon on a bicycle was just one moment, in just one lifetime. A moment like every other one, like every other morning when the clock sounds and we push aside the covers and dare to live as if we were wholly and completely alive.[40]

To Repair with Gold

Resilience. Grit.[41] *Sisu.*[42] Post traumatic growth.[43] Different researchers emphasize the subtle distinctions within the larger truth that more often than not, we are better than we think we are.[44] We are stronger, more adaptive. When things go wrong, most people, most of the time, do not dry up, crumble and fall to pieces. We are better able to withstand the disappointments and tragedies, hardships and tempests that rage during the span of our all-to-human lives.

When trauma does occur, rude and unexpected, it often cuts at our very foundations. It disrupts the most fundamental truths we'd held about our time on this earth. We want to believe that the world is good and just and beautiful and fair and we go about ordering our lives as such. And then one of the inconvenient, inconsiderate facts of our lives happens. A tumor awakes in a rage while we are eating casserole at the PTA potluck. Or the boy who used to chase soccer balls into your flower garden, doesn't come home one night after the high school dance. Or after building a life's worth of dreams with that special someone who once upon a time gazed in your eyes and promised to be there until death do you part, you discover that they had another life

73

and other dreams and everything upon which you had ordered your life, is left in shambles. Trauma undermines the narrative we have of our lives and robs us of cohesion and meaning.

And as we stand there in the hazy aftermath, heart and spirit both raw, we are somehow supposed to keep going on with our regular lives. We are expected to make sense of the anemic normalcy of the shopping mall, or standing in lines going nowhere, or all of the planned and unplanned obsolesces we are told we want.

Some people never really recover.

However the good news is that research shows most people navigate the hardships just fine. They are the ones you see every day in the lunch room, or the next cubical at work. Maybe they move a little more slowly, as if they have some sort of psychological limp. But after the suffering and struggling, most cope and rise again to live lives of simple happiness.

But even this is not the whole story. When the hardships happen, when life kicks the legs of the stool out from under us, there are some people who find a way to build new foundations and a new story.

In Japan there is an art form called *kintsukuroi* which means "to repair with gold".[45] When a ceramic pot or bowl would break, the artisan would put the pieces together again using gold or silver lacquer to create something stronger, more beautiful, then it was before. The breaking is not something to hide. It does not mean that the work of art is ruined or without value because it is different than what was planned. *Kintsukuroi* is a way of living that embraces every flaw and imperfection. Every crack is part of the history of the object and it becomes more beautiful, precisely because it had been broken.

People are the same way.

Sometimes, when everything we valued and built up and cared for over the years falls to pieces, we are better able to see opportunities and possibilities that would have never presented themselves had life not been torn to rags. Or standing and staring in the face of broken promises and broken dreams, eye-to-bloodshot-eye with our most assiduous fears, sometimes we discover that we were stronger than we imagined: that we can withstand more and that there is no reason to fear. Sometimes trauma brings us closer to God, or to our purpose in life, or leaves us more appreciative than we were before: appreciative and even happy. And when we are betrayed by someone we've loved, or taken advantage of, sometimes it is our trust and faith in others that grows stronger. We look around at all the friends and acquaintances and strangers that come rushing to our aide, and our faith in human goodness is restored. Cherish your relationships. Nurture them.

The fact that some people grow under strain is not cause for self-flagellation in the midst of pain. It does not undermine the difficulties of living a hard life, or mean we would simply "get over it" by thinking happy thoughts.

After losing his three-year-old child, Rabbi Harold Kushner wrote he was a better counselor, and a better spiritual guide. He was wiser, more forgiving, and had greater patience. And yet, Kushner continued, he would have given it all up - the growth, the strength, the wizened gaze - if only he could have his child back, or could have avoided the pain.[46]

That people are resilient is neither a stick of admonishment, nor a salve that takes suffering away. What it is, is a marker of hope. People can grow in the face of the horrific. It is evidence of what might be possible, no matter the loss, no matter the pain.

Learning to Ride a Bicycle

When my children where first learning to ride a bicycle, I would take them to a field behind the school, or out to the park, where the grass would be forgiving of tender elbows and knees. Their excitement was tactile, honest. With rapt attention, my daughter kicked her leg up over the seat: self-confident but with enough nervousness to make her attentive. How could I expect her to know any risks beyond rumors of skinned knees? Risks that I, grown wise and timid, saw behind every dandelion and buttercup. Holding her and her bike firmly, I began to run. Slowly at first with a steadying hand, but increasing in momentum as she peddled faster and faster.

This scene has of course, passed. All my children are grown now. My joints no longer allow me to chase behind bicycles. And while the memory perches in my mind like a nightingale on a green branch, it too will fade as silently as a bird passing on its way to the horizon.

Yet these are the moments that make me believe that permanence is possible. Ceremonies of innocence happen unscripted every day. In every country, every era, *Innocence* - chaste, guiltless - unclasps its hands and lets our children loose into the uncertainty.

I never wanted to let go. I never did let go. Exuberant and determined, my daughter peddled harder and harder and pulled away from me. She wobbled and swerved into the future with confidence and grace. There is nothing about a parent's fear that can ever change that.

Permanence is not this one moment on a bicycle. The facts of the different time and different place vary and prove unimportant. Maybe it was that boy sailing ships in the *Jardin du Luxembourg*, using his wooden stick to navigate salty oblivion. Or maybe that girl in a long dress, tossing and catching the inflated bladder of a pig, forever preserved in oil by some Dutch master. Our children touch the things of death so lightly and yet their smiles require no translation. The dangers I fear are real. They exist in the vacant lots where boys in dust-rag shirts swing cricket bats as if there were no other joy. And they are there on the city streets filled with strangers: the same streets and same strangers given music by the child pressing bottle caps to the bottoms of his sneakers to make tap shoes and beg for coins. And the worst torments of all are the internal fears and doubts and self-criticisms invisible to my protective gaze. When little girls who believe in pig tails run, please let it always be to kick a crushed soda can overflowing with laughter and dreams. That afternoon in the park with my daughter was one of the immortal moments given me, timeless, fleeting, but that provides luminance between two everlasting darknesses.

How many more times would I have to watch or imagine as she goes forward in a world that doesn't always have soft fields to break her fall? When she pulled away balanced on a bicycle she did not look back over her shoulder. But letting go does not have to mean having to go it alone.

The whole of my life has been about learning this balance. In my teens and early twenties, I felt an existential howl deep in my bones. No one could ever know me. No one could ever feel what I felt. The face I showed to the world was only what was safe and expected, but could never reveal those deep things inside me that no one could ever accept. I was as anxious to be free as a child on a bicycle, but chained in my own aloneness.

As I got older I discovered I was not alone. I discovered that love was not about me, or whether some "she" returned my gaze. The joys of a child on a bicycle completed me and filled whatever holes I thought were in my character and in my soul.

But now my temples grey, I did not expect this new, deeper aloneness. Alone and helpless, having to watch the ones you love navigate the hardness of the world. For the universe is thick with harsh things that no child, no one, should ever have to face or confront.

With unbounding innocence, my daughter imagines herself ready for what lay beyond the horizon. And yet I know it is too big. I am an optimist and will forever believe in the inherent goodness of people, yet I know the world is too unforgiving. At some point in our lives, between seventy and ninety percent of us will experience a traumatic event. Forty-three percent of kids have already done so before they turn eighteen. Someone is sexually assaulted in the US every two minutes. Teen depression and psychopathology has risen five-fold since the early part of the 20th century.

In India, there is a belief that when a child is born some god or goddess comes down and writes the details of its life on its forehead. Every joy. Every spider bite. If I could only see. Which of the facts of her destiny would I try to erase? Which sufferings would build her up, and which pleasures bring her down? As if somehow, I could guarantee for her a world that was fair and just and always kind.

But I cannot see, and a new aloneness creeps in. There is nothing about life or trauma or suffering that scares me. I have learned that I am strong enough to withstand any hardship. But what of the hardships that do not befall me? What of those traumas that slip from the fingertips of the cosmos as unevenly as ash spread by a dove at sunset?

What can we do? The world is the world regardless of what I think or hope or pray. If I can no longer stand behind my children steadying them what can I do?

Let them know that you love them. Let them know that whatever secrets they hold, whatever impure thoughts they have had or deeds they've done, that nothing can dull their luster.

Let them know that they are more than one thought, or one moment or one mistake. Let them know that whatever bad things happened, nothing can bind their present or corrupt their future. Their lives and happiness are not dictated by events or the past.

Teach them that bad things will happen to them in life. The world is filled with many things, and many of those things are terrible. It is not fair. We might not understand why. But teach them to always, always look for what good they can take from whatever life hands them. Because there will always be something that can help nurture and strengthen them. Maybe they will discover that they are stronger than they thought they were; better able to cope; better able to hold others afloat. "What could life ever do to me now after I have lived through this?" Maybe when bad things happen they will notice the unexpected people who rush to their aid and comfort. It will not always be those they expected, but there are always helpers. We are not alone after all. It is just that the angels in our lives might not be known to us in this moment. Maybe in the face of something horrible they will find the grace and strength and insight to rewrite the story of their lives to be one of coherence and clarity and even kindness. Maybe they will realize that many of the things that they thought were important really do not matter. Because they have learned of their power to infuse kindness and hope and meaning into the lives of others.

Help them – your children, your spouse, those you love - to see that they are more humanly perfect than they believe. Let them know that they complete you.

Permanence is not some unbroken chain in my consciousness or memory or understanding. It cannot be plotted out on some line graph or spreadsheet. All of us participate in a serial permanence – the same struggles, the same traumas, the same joys – that have always been with us. And all of us have the power to find meaning and relief and

81

happiness in our lives, by creating meaning and relief and happiness in the lives of those around us.

Sardines

From May to July each year, off the southern coast of Africa, hundreds of millions of sardines move north from the Agulhas Bank toward Mozambique. These shoals are often more than five miles long, a mile wide and 100 feet deep and can be seen from surface and sky. This glimmering mass of exhales ignites a feeding frenzy among copper sharks and bronze whalers, bluefish and mackerel, cormorants and terns. Cape Fur Seals follow the shoals up the coastline as far as Port St. Johns.

And for these poor pilchards drunk from their spawning, death came unseen: grouper and garrick, geelbeck and dolphin surging upward from beneath. Cape Gannets by the thousands plunging into the sea. With every dive, every violent spearing, each headlong splash down and lunge into the surf, another of the shining innocents was gone. And the sardines can do nothing but cluster and swim and watch.

We are that cloud that dances beneath the surface in sequins. We never know who among us will be struck with dementia or crushed in a car accident. Strokes never come when it's convenient. Stable marriages dissolve as easily as trust, and it is not strangers who are raped by strangers.

These gannets and sharks and chance never heard of karma or justice. They did not look for the irresponsible. They did not single out the reckless ones or those who tempted fate. With the selectivity of cancer they simply choose. They choose the young neighbor down the block who just gave birth to her second child. Or that gentle man in the office you've sat next to for thirteen years. They picked your running buddy, exuberant and inspiring. The one you could count on to be there in the park at 6:00 a.m., until one day he wasn't. His absence was only surprising because of the untimely normalcy.

Tragedy is what is whispered in rumors about your old roommate, or quietly screamed by your best friend's eyes. It roughly shoves that kindergartener who was swinging on the playground every Sunday after Sunday after church. When it came time to choose, *Fate*, like a spinner shark, selected the mothers and fathers and children who had nothing but lives and wishes and dreams.

You look around and ask yourself "why"? Why was I the one who was spared? I am not the best of the lot. When there is so such about my life, terrible things, embarrassing things, that I can never share, why am I the one who was pardoned? Of those who were plucked from the shoal, not one among them felt anonymous. To their families and neighbors swimming furiously alongside them, they were not simply one of the infinite identical. They were special, unique. For every one of them, it felt like life mattered and that made the hardship feel personal. The gulls eat their fill and we can just keep swimming and swimming and swimming.

The whole of my life has been a back-and-forth between finding balance between our inherent aloneness and the love and oneness with others. In my teens and early twenties I felt as isolated as an artic flow. No one could ever know me. No one would ever understand who I was or see the dark truths that I could never reveal. I swam in perfect unison with the shoal because that was all I and they could ever accept.

But later, sometime much later, I discovered something. There were many times I had felt that feeding frenzy in my heart and thought I understood love and happiness. But it took the still pools and faint reflections to recognize the deep truth that love was caring for another more than I cared for myself. My life mattered because there was something that mattered more than me.

But just as a blacktip shark rises up from the sea floor, tragedy will strike the ones you love. You lock the doors at night. You teach them about strangers. You make them eat their vitamins and their vegetables and you realize that no matter what you did, how much you cared, how hard you loved, that there was nothing you could do to shield them from the whims of the world. The tempered bolts on the door can only keep out so much. They cannot protect against dormant tumors that awake in a rage and do not discriminate. They cannot ward off *Fate* with its charm bracelet of illness, accidents and indiscretions. The lock on the door cannot stop those violations of trust that make us question whether goodness is even possible. And no lock can protect our loved ones from the most terrifying phantoms of all, those that haunt from within: depression, despair, self-doubt and thoughts of self-harm. I was deeply, deeply in love and was even more helpless than before, watching tragedies I wished were my own.

I realize my history and that of my clan. I have steeled myself against the horrors of the world and have seen what hardships I have endured. I am not afraid of life. I know I can resist any adversity. I thought I overcame my fate and the prophecies writ within my genes. But what are we to do when the hardship happen to the ones we love? When the internal demons are not our own, but belong to our spouse or sibling, our child or friend? A Bryde's whale lunges to the surface with its jaws wide.

I am old enough to know that life is not fair. It spreads injustice equality and adorns itself in paradox, incongruence, and irony. The things that occur, the things that do not occur, there is so much about life that is too personal and too painful. And so there are two great truths about the world that we must learn if we are to maintain our health, our happiness and our sanity.

The first is acceptance. Accept that when life happens that we might never understand why. When a child is abducted or an organ fails, when bacteria sneaks in and infects while we were watching something else, when psychosis subtly slips past the net of diagnosis and comprehension, what are we to do? We can declare the world tragic. We can develop theories about human nature or banish these rude facts to the edges of awareness. We can blame the other or blame ourselves. We can even blame God or the absence of a god. But the simple truth is we might never understand "why." It is bad enough when traumas simply slip unattended from the lining of fate. But the pain is particularly acute when there is someone else, someone we know, someone we love, who helped cause the suffering. Or someone who knows what happened - perpetrator or witness or victim - but will not say. They might have their reasons. They may have dressed the trauma in the gown of forgetfulness. They might be trying to protect another, more innocent, innocent. Or they simply may not be prepared to stare in the face of a fate that is too big for all of us. These ones, the quiet ones, have their pain too.

So when hardship happens to the ones we love, we must accept that we might never understand "why." Our sanity, our health and happiness demand it.

Of course, there is a chance that what seems so clouded now will become clear in a week. Maybe we will understand it in a month or two. Maybe it will take ten months or twelve years. We might have to wade through decades of lingering effects before the truth becomes known. But this is why there are piers that extend into the sea and provide grounding for old men and old women as weathered and grey as a mooring we'd trust our tethers too. Fate is not measured by its depth or breadth or the consequences we fear. Every trial, every trauma that rolled in and tormented over a long life receded back again, mimicking the tide. And as we look behind us over the horizon, the sea reveals itself as calm.

Be patient. Do what you must to keep kicking and swimming and taking air into your lungs, but accept that you might never understand.

The second essential truth is a realization: A realization that it is o.k. if we never understand. The world is so much bigger than we are, and we are not equipped to process everything. Tragedy may feel personal. It may cut at the very foundations of everything we have ever believed about the goodness of people, the beauty of life, or the benevolence of God. But this void we call our universe and home is pregnant with so much goodness and beauty and magnificence, yet it is not goodness or beauty or magnificence. So to, it is filled with evil and pain and suffering, but the world is not evil or pain or suffering. It is, as a system, complete. I stand amid the tide trying to divine a fate that comes to me in waves. For so much in life, there is no answer. This pulsing surf cannot tell me what I should do. But that does not delay the sea from its flowing over the sand and shells and rocks, smoothing them and purifying itself over and over again.

The Exquisite Tapestry

Memories never reveal what actually happened. They obscure as much as they preserve, leaving only a sense. The sense of those early days was that life was meant to be smelled and tasted and touched. So, with the girl who lived next door and the boy from down the block, we ran in the yard, splashed through rain-filled ditches and skinned our knees on the maple and willow tress we climbed. We crawled out of windows and snuck cookies from the jar. Toy soldiers tumbled down the laundry chute, and we even played in her father's bedroom while he was dying.

As the old man's exhales escorted him toward death, we would hide-and-seek in the closets, ducking our heads beneath overcoats. Or I would pick through his tall basket of walking sticks, or run my finger across the smooth, carved pipes on his dresser. The smell of tobacco lingered with them, wooden and sweet. He had a great grey mustache, and on the top shelf, the type of hat that went with canes.

It did not seem strange to play so close to a dying man. He had a patience and understanding I had never known. It was a calm vulnerability and contentment that as a child I could not name. Dr. Davis was a psychologist. His adult daughter was mentally handicapped and from the yard I could hear her screams at night. I suppose he had seen so much of life that he didn't mind little boys and girls running through the room with their mischief and laughter.

But of all of the magnificent things in the house, there was the great, wooden loom beside his bed. Its mahogany shine and innumerable strings were even more magical than patience or death.

It is said that among the immortals, only the goddesses were weavers. In Japan there was the grateful crane, who after being rescued and set free, came back as bride to her poor farmer-hero. In secret, she wove the most delicate cloth for him out of her own white feathers, leaving nothing behind.[47]

And there was the Chinese weaver goddess who spun the stars and the starlight.[48] Or on long summer days, Saulé wove the sunbeams to brighten her Baltic landscapes.[49]

Meanwhile as Dawn stretched her rosy fingers out over a vacant sea, Penelope wove and waited. There was neither news nor rumor of her husband, of his homecoming, of whether he survived the war or was drowned at sea. And so when the shafts of sun were put away each night, she unraveled everything, to prevent the fates she could not bear.[50]

But there are some pasts and futures we cannot unravel, so we embroider them as best we can. Dr. Davis wove the blanket at the foot of his bed and the blouse his daughter wore. Everything, the wall hangings and scarves, the throw rugs, were all covered with delicate birds, flowers and creatures from the forest. There were banquets of homecoming. Horsemen in their hunting grounds, sacred and primal.

And with their faithfulness and honor, knights who promised to silence the dragon's howl. The room was a place a wonder, and I discovered gratitude there.

We know that gratitude is good for us. [51] People who are grateful are healthier and feel better about their lives.[52] They make greater progress toward goals, are optimistic and more likely to help others.[53] When we are grateful, we are more forgiving, empathic and agreeable.[54] Overall, gratitude means purpose[55] and satisfaction with life.[56]

But when the sadness happens, it doesn't help that we "know" that gratitude is good for us. We may try to find and treasure the good things, only to become even more beaten down. We put pressure on ourselves and feel that we can't even get gratitude right.

Or when things fall apart, and all our well-meaning loved ones point to the everyday, normal blessings and insist that we "should" feel grateful, it just sounds ignorant, insensitive and naive.

How are we to feel grateful after we'd lost the thing that mattered most? Where does gratitude come from when we pick up the paper and see that all of the horrors of history are happening now - genocide and terror, environmental holocaust, children who are abused and the innocent laid bare?

Whitman looked at the ugly and crass and called it beautiful. Aghori sadhus see everything in life as holy, even death and defecation. Could it be that beauty and holiness are only possible when the suffering is impersonal? We sigh and exhale a vague nostalgia that blankets the pain of living. Or maybe we can only see the quotidian-divine when we look in the other's eyes and offer something human. Maybe it is the humanity, not the suffering, that is beautiful. But where does the gratitude fit in?[57]

So I try to learn to accept, to accept and to fight, and to accept again. I accept that life and death and sickness and blight and famine exist. I can fight like hell against injustice. I can care for the sick, or sell my shirt to feed the hungry. I can provide individual moments of comfort to those who share my small corner of eternity. I can do all of this while at the same time knowing that my efforts are small, limited in time and space and scope against the background of forever.[58] History has a long tail and she swings it without discretion. I can accept and fight and accept, but is gratefulness really possible?

It seems there are three layers to gratitude.

The first involves perspective. In the midst of misfortune and difficulty, it is healthy and transformative to recognize how blessed we are, even with our troubles. Frustration about a job becomes gratefulness and pride that you are able provide safety and comfort for your family. The financial strain that can feel so crushing, dissolves, when we recognize there are whole nations of children without shelter or safety or bread. Gratitude is about appreciating what you *do* have.

The second layer involves benefit. Suffering is rarely as painful as we expect. It does not last as long as we feared. And whether soapstone or ivory, hardships bring with them unforeseen gifts. Often they are no more than trinkets we'd rather throw away. But sometimes, every now and then, after the divorce, in the wake of the bankruptcy, or when that job you needed was lost, epiphanies emerge, green and beautiful, precisely where the foundations had cracked.

While these sorts of gratitude are adaptive and mature, there is another level that reaches deeper and touches us more fully. A sort of gratitude that is neither a salve for our discontent nor love for what tragedy gives us.

As we played there in the room, sometimes Dr. Davis would ask me to choose my favorite colors. I picked through the threads on the countertop and there were certain ones I always loved and wanted. There was a red, the first hue to fade into twilight like a bride's warm blush. Or the yellow of bees giving gifts of combs and honey from all my old failures[59]. And there were the threads of violet and indigo and the quiet, humble saffron, filled with the hope and longing of every aspirant and suitor, and of the poet who announces the age of the moon.[60] Each thread was pure and pristine onto itself. It was as if we had found the happiness we had longed for wound round each single, wooden spool. A happiness we could slip into our pockets forever, or hold lightly in our palm to stretch and trace the line of our joy out into eternity whenever we wanted.

Why have we come to expect that we should only feel one emotion, fully and honestly, at any single point in time? How a wedding should offer us nothing but bliss? Or a death, nothing but pain? As though, if any other feeling were to creep in, it would betray our love, or dishonor our grief.

Yet when the wedding day comes, and we see our daughter filled with joy and love, and beautiful in her hope, we cannot help but also feel the loss and sadness and fear. Or when all the mourners and strangers to the corpse have assembled in the pews, a distant cousin rises, stands strong in her sadness and tells how she and he used to sneak away from their jobs to practice the latest dance. This would not be our only loss. Throughout our lives we are handed hardships with opened palms. We withstand tragedies. Tens of thousands of tangible and intangible things dissolve. Yet sixty years later and a loved one dead and gone, there was nothing in the church that day except laughter and smiles and beauteous reminiscences.

I'll always love life's tender moments, warm and soft as pashmina. The spools of azure down, resembling mountain pools and reflected sky. Or a mother's joy at the birth of her son, how he entered the world with his eyes wide and absorbing. But no matter how delicate or lustrous, it is not the individual, sparkling strands that give the blouses and tapestries their splendor.

So too, it is salty tears with their eternal moisture. It is the love, and the ache that only comes with love. It is anger and frustration and memories of laughter. The magnificence of our lives is found in every regret that we have ever had, too. Like the carpet of Solomon[61] firm beneath our feet, the magic of our lives exists because of the full texture and balance, the context and unity, and all of the beautiful disorder. The only ironic thing is that irony does not matter. The majesty is found by holding all of these things at the exact same time, the contrary and contradictory, the wholly unholy and unfair and the relentlessly beautiful.

Those who can hold the positive and negative at the same time are the most resilient,[62] no matter how acute the stress or how deep the pain. Any one moment may fill us completely with love and anger and deep and honest despair. Like a Homeric hero, our son or spouse or neighbor or boss may evoke annoyance, disgust, frustration and rage. Yet the love runs deep, or the admiration or the awe. Or all of them at the same time. We can embrace the full emotive spectrum of our lives and continue to function. We must. We can look at the hopelessness of our plight and insist on nothing but hope. We must. [63]

This is not some naive pretense of one who dreams. Rather, it is finding the perfection inherent in the flawed. It is the humbly grateful recognition that we are each part of it all, as essential to the landscape as the foaming dogwoods or the dew dropping dawn. We are as a much part of this silk tapestry of dreams as the jewel-pocked Phoenix rising up over tulips and water lilies, as is befitting the majesty of kings.

So there is a third sort of gratitude. Greater. Softer. More accepting and transcendent. A sort of gratitude that does not depend upon finding the "the bright side" of things, or blessing us with an "opportunity to grow".[64] It is a peace and wholeness that does not shy away from any of the parts of life. Not from the pain or grief, the sadness or despair, or even the hopelessness. It goes about embracing the beauty, the joy, the miracle and gift of being alive, while standing fully and completely in the sadness or pain. It is a gratitude in the face of a diagnosis. Not "for" the cancer or curse, never. But a gratitude that we are part of it all, essential to the magnificent tapestry. We can never disentangle the beautiful from the painful and plain. There can be "no worship, no music, no love," Rabi Heschel taught, "if we take for granted the blessings or defeats of living."[65]

That goddess from the Tang Dynasty, the one who floated down on a shaft of moonlight: her gown was wholly without seams. Just as the silk tapestry of our lives is beautiful, comprehensive and simply perfect.

Part IV. Embracing it All

Earthworms and Puddles

In the midst of the unrest, turbulence and protests of what would be called the "Arab Spring", I had the privilege of working with a government group in the Middle East on issues of happiness and well-being. It rained every day. Yet everyone I met, commented how beautiful it was.

At first, I thought they were being facetious. In the US, most people complain about rainy days. But this was different. When they spoke, there was no cynicism in their eyes. There was no complaint in their shoulders or their arms. They were genuinely tickled that it was raining. When it only rains nine days a year, those days are pretty special. They are something to celebrate.

Once upon a time before I was so busy, and professional and wearing suits, I too loved the rain. I walked to school without an umbrella, head thrown back, and let the universe soak me. As a young father I would drag my feet through the puddles with my four-year-old son as he collected the earthworms that had come out, and put them in his pockets to protect them from the birds. The rain presented opportunities for awe. It was an invitation to rainbows and freshness and majesty. Those opportunities are still there, all around us, as they have always been since the beginning. And yet we miss them.

We are just so busy. We have been taught that we can have whatever we want, be whatever we want, as long as we work hard enough. And so we work. And yet this neighbor has a bigger house, that one a better title and the one around the corner vacations in more fabulous venues. And so we work and are less satisfied.

Our children are working too. As loving parents, we want the very best for them. We want to give them every opportunity we can. There is just so much to offer, so much that would be good for them to experience and enjoy. We fill their lives with soccer practice and piano and Spanish lessons and art classes and summer camp. We help them build water rockets for the science fair and take them to math tutors so they don't fall behind those cubs of the tiger moms.

Individually, these are all good things. In studies, children who are engaged and active are happier than those who dawdle their time away at the mall, or who wrap their heads around a video screen. We would feel like failures and neglectful parents if we didn't do for our children everything we could. Yet by giving them everything, there is something we are missing. We are losing something essential, something vital to our health, happiness and well-being.

CBS news reports that each week more Americans take antidepressants than go to the movies. Rates of depression and anxiety among young people have been rising for over fifty years. Today five to eight times more high school and college students meet the criteria for major depression or anxiety disorders than half a century ago.

Even if we are not the one in ten Americans experiencing clinical levels of depression, all of this running around, striving and strain has us stretched thin and stressed out. Stanford neurobiologist Robert Sapolsky points out that stress is a normal, life-saving strategy when it consists of "three minutes of screaming terror on the savannah" when we are fleeing a predator.[66] After that either the stress response is over or we are. During those three minutes, the body focuses all its energies on responding to the immediate threat. It releases stress hormones to raise the heart rate and blood pressure to pump the blood where it is needed. Stress also turns off those functions that are not needed in that moment of crisis, such as digestion, growth and reproduction.

Yet, when we experience pressing deadlines at work, stress over the economy, a screaming baboon of a boss, anxiety at how to get our daughter from volleyball to voice lessons while our son is at soccer across town, our bodies secrete the exact same hormones as it would if a lion were chasing us across the savanna. This stress response is on all day. By not being able to shut off this adaptive and effective defense, stress wreaks havoc on our bodies and in our lives. It increases the onset of diabetes and high blood pressure. It sets us up for gastrointestinal disorders and adversely affects the way fat is distributed in our bodies. Stress diminishes brain cells and measurably accelerates the aging of our chromosomes.

Plus with all this frantic running around, we are not having fun. It is not the busyness that is killing us. It is o.k. to be active and engaged. But by rushing to squeeze in everything, so often we squeeze out the joy. If in our mad rush, we don't get the kids to swim lessons on time, we torment ourselves. It is this impatience that is the source of the stress. We need to slow down.

Slowing down reenergizes us and allows us to nurture ourselves so we can enjoy what we are doing in the moment we are doing it. It allows us to connect with people, rather than just check in. It opens us to awe and wonder, and lets us play and discover the beauty that exists all around us. By being more deliberate, we can better evaluate what things connect most directly with our values. By so doing, slowing down gives us the consciousness and mettle to say "no" to things that might be really good, and that we really want to do, but that keep us from our most essential purpose.

But how? If you are a solution-oriented problem solver, someone who tackles every challenge head on, the real challenge is in not tackling. How do you dial back or let your foot off the pedal? In survival literature, an essential aspect to withstanding tragedies, accidents and natural disasters is in knowing when not to act, when to be "actively passive". We must avoid the urge to do something, simply because "doing" feels productive. How do we, in the midst of chaos, maintain our calm, enjoy the ride, and see what possibilities present themselves?

The great promise of technology is to make things easier for us. Ask yourself, what things do you consciously do to make life harder? What rituals have you established to force yourself to slow down?

Devout Muslims stop their world five times a day. They step out of business meetings. Restaurants close. City buses stop. All so the businessmen, cooks and bus drivers can kneel upon the ground and shift their focus to something bigger than themselves.

For others, meditation has remarkable benefits. Years of research has demonstrated that the mindfulness achieved from meditation increases happiness, effectiveness and our ability to connect. When we are mindful we become less judgmental, our memory and attention improve, and rates of burnout decrease. The literature even suggests that meditation may allow us to live longer.

Meditation is not the only pathway to mindfulness. In her work, Harvard psychologist Ellen Langer finds that we can enjoy many of the same benefits by simply becoming more aware and adopting processes of noticing new things.

One way might be through poetry. Poetry forces you to look at familiar things in new ways. Adam Zagajewski forever changed the way I see sunsets and life by pointing out that "Sometimes the sun's coin dims/and life shrinks so small/that you could tuck it/in the blue gloves of the Gypsy".[67]

Awareness can be cultivated through other arts as well. Artist Ali Sobel-Read[68] constantly scans the near horizon for old bits of tires, plastic netting and other refuge, for the beauty their patterns might bring into her art. For others, slowing down might consist of working in the garden. To plant a seed and nurture to bloom, to feel the damp soil between our fingers, gets us in touch with the earth's eternal rhythm.

Every time we take a bite, or prepare a meal, we have a chance to savor and slow down. Take something as simple as an onion, "clear as a planet/and destined/to shine". Every one of our five senses is wholly engaged in cooking this "luminous flask". Feel the hard coolness in your palm, the texture as you cut across the across the grain. Smell the sweet burn before mixing it in warm olive oil and completing a holy trinity with bell pepper and celery. Of the onion Neruda said, "You make us cry without hurting us."[69] Certain foods have a transcendent effect. When we become aware that we are sharing in a primordial staple celebrated by the peoples of ancient Egypt, Mesopotamia and the Indus Valley, we are transported across time and space and are more tightly woven into the fabric of the human history.

But we need not eclipse the present to find calm and peace through connection. Simply take time for a friend. Sit on the porch with your elderly neighbor, play backgammon or Parcheesi and watch the day take on the pace of a rocking chair. Or walk out your front door into nature. Take off your shoes or lie in the grass to reconnect with the earth we've forgotten. Look up at the sky at the same birds and squirrels in the same trees you see around you every day. But notice the new dimensions, the new horizons that are born, from lying horizontal in the grass. There is an acrobatic wonder taking place right above you, just outside your everyday awareness. Or even go out and walk in the rain.

Secret Destinations

Each of us have certain needs. If we are to feel secure in the world, grounded and fulfilled, various human imperatives must be met. Some involve safety or companionship. Others concern healthy attachments,[70] and feelings of competence and significance.[71] We want to know that we belong,[72] and that our lives matter in some way.[73]

We have individual needs too. Curious, reflective, I frequently have to find some quiet space so I can clear my head and regain my bearings. And when the tangible things upon which I depend breakdown - the computer, the car, my health - it takes energy for me to maintain my center and focus so I can keep moving forward.

But because this world is a world outside of our control, there is great benefit in sometimes letting go of precisely those things we think we need.[74] One way to practice at letting go, is travel.

Whether travel opens us to things that are authentically unintelligible or surprisingly mundane and familiar, true travel requires us to let go of our provincial expectations and see what actually "is". By seeking out that which is strange, exotic and foreign, or that disrupts our expectations, we can upset our balance and regain our equilibrium. By inserting ourselves into foreign environments where the rules are not clear and deliberately distancing ourselves from those things we thought we needed, we can rediscover who we really are and how to live life more passionately. If we can allow ourselves to be patient, let things happen at their own pace, and learn to laugh at our own presumptions, it opens us to a sense of awe and wonder and appreciation that has almost been lost to our time. And because we are always growing, always changing and always adapting, we should travel often. We should regularly seek to deprive ourselves of the familiar and frequently upset our own balance.

When life thrusts the unfamiliar upon us, our character becomes confused and vulnerable to influence. It causes good Stanford college kids to act as ruthlessly as prison guards.[75] Gentle fathers become torturers from Auschwitz to Abu Ghraib,[76] and neighbors bolt their windows to a faceless victim's screams.[77] Sitting outside the safe-familiar leads churchgoing men in shirt sleeves to turn the dial so many clicks so as to deliver a deadly shock,[78] and airline passengers to obediently stay buckled in their seats while the plane burns around them.[79]

But the unfamiliar also reveals saints and heroes in our midst. It causes mothers to risk the safety of their own children by hiding Jews, Tutsis, or Bosnia's Muslims and Croats, regardless of whether they are neighbor or stranger. "How else can we bring ourselves to look our own children in the face?", they ask. When the structure of our lives is so consumed in flames we would have thought we were in hell, there is always someone who runs back into the fire, because they know there are others who will perish if left on their own. Bodhisattvas reject eternal bliss. Angels remind us of the messages we need. Men leave their children on the platform as they dive on the railroad tracks to rescue a stranger. And everywhere we find someone who really believes when Christ said, "If you wish to be complete, go and sell your possessions and give to the poor. . .".

Who among us wants to be complete? Who are these Samaritans we all wish to be? They do not possess anything superhuman. They are not demi-gods or omnipotent. However somehow, they are able to stand in the unfamiliar and, with clear heads, choose. They choose actions based upon that which would be the best for the world and best for one other. A man's character is not only "his" fate, as Heraclites said, but it dictates the fate of everyone around him.

And so, are we left to the whims of a fickle and unjust universe? When fortunes shift, am I helpless to the acoustics rapt out by my own character knocking? It is true that part of who I am runs backwards through time and space like an invisible scarlet thread linking me to a certain history and temperament and preferences common to my tribe.

But there is another truth too. We become what we do. Character is shaped by action. And we can prepare for uncertainty and change by rehearsing our lines within uncertainty and change. If we practice at being off-balance, then we can learn to bring out our best when assaulted with the unfamiliar. When the world is suddenly tipped up on its end and all the sense shaken out of it, we must still respond. This is the way life works. One day you will be in the middle of your routine, so busy with so many important things to do, and the solid ground upon which you have stood for decades will crumble dry as dust. There will be no notice. There is no vaccination or immunity against a relapse of instability. The only thing we can do for our health, growth and flourishing is practice at being off balance and learn the deep heart lessons of humor and humility, appreciation and acceptance, gratitude and grace. This is essential for us as individuals. It is essential for us as a people.

To deliberately invite this healing chaos and uncertainty, we must walk out to the edges of our world. We must look out to our horizons – be they visual, auditory, taste, touch, smell, cultural, linguistic - and test whether what we thought was true runs beyond the limits of our gaze

Travel is one such way to stretch ourselves beyond ourselves. It can prepare us for this impermanence, and for the decline, death and decay of both body and expectations as we simultaneously feel ourselves the most alive. Travel can be to places half-way around globe, or half-way around the block. It is not measured by frequent flyer miles, the number of stamps in our passports, or world wonders seen. The quality and volume of the world seen is assessed through the disrupted assumptions. It occurs when we meet people where they live and touch those things most precious, most personal and most essential to their lives. It is through contact that we spark an internal renaissance that enriches our lives and spans the oceans between us and our neighbors.

But for most of us travel has become something different: Antiseptic; Familiar; Pleasant; Relaxing. The natives become "mimics of themselves" and are placed with camels or monkeys where the tour books told us we would find them.[80] Our vacations are as comfortable as a stroll from the drawing room to the parlor. There was a time when travel meant no newspapers or Internet, satellite phones or Skype. There were no antibiotics to evict unwelcomed microbes from our guts. There were no translators, or spas with elliptical machines and hot yoga, no peppermint scalp massages. There was a time when travel did not mean five-star resorts, let alone private beds. To sleep meant to share a mattress and rough wool blanket with bedbugs, fleas and whatever human pests the innkeeper assigned.[81] Travel meant rationing fresh water and risking disease. Of course, I do appreciate modern ease and safety. But we have lost something essential when we complain that the cab driver speaks with a heavy accent, or that there are not enough towels by the hotel pool.

No. For the salvation of our souls, we must travel and encounter people where they live. Discover what they hold most dear or find to be the most precious. True travel is not about pock-marked ruins or scrolls rescued from a barbarian's fire. True travel means to go to that place and touch those things that provide significance for the inward lives of people.

Adventures Just Outside Your Door

Your world is a world of wonder. There is so much right outside your door waiting for you, waiting to lead you to where the awe comes from, to the inspiration and humility. By going out of our way and looking for discomfort or taking those gentle risks, we break up our usual routines. These "microadventures" allow us to see our everyday world differently. They need not be big or grand, dangerous or far from home. But every now and then we should go out and interrupt the normalcy.

Alastair Humphreys, the 2012 National Geographic Adventurer of the Year, describes microadventures as any sort of adventure that is "short, simple, local, cheap – yet still fun, exciting, challenging, refreshing and rewarding."[82] He offers examples. Follow a river to its source. Take a train or a bus to a new town, spend the day there and cycle back. After work, go wild camping and stargazing and then, in the morning, watch the sunrise before heading back to the office. Doing so will offer new perspectives to a familiar place.

When we seek the strange or exotic that is just outside our door, we disrupt our expectations. We put ourselves off balance and regain our equilibrium.[83] By deliberately inserting ourselves into places where the rules are not clear, or where we lack what we thought we needed, we can rediscover who we really are and begin to live our lives more passionately.

It is about learning to play again. In the pantheon of human virtues, "zest", that wholeheartedness of living, has a robust connection to a deep satisfaction in life.[84] Yet while our children exhibit it naturally and beautifully, somewhere along the line most of us lose this flower-laden path to happiness and fulfillment.[85] We were just so busy growing up and struggling to establish who we are.

To throw ourselves into the world, into the surprising and uncomfortable, is an invitation to laugh at our own presumptions. When we discover for the first time what was right before our eyes, it opens us to the wonder of living. And because we are always growing, always changing and adapting, we should release ourselves into the unfamiliar and new again and again and again.

The opportunities for play and for awe are all around us. We need only look to the edges of our everyday lives, to our horizons – be they visual, auditory, taste, touch, smell, cultural, linguistic - and then press to see what runs beyond the limits of our gaze.[86]

Maybe it is climbing the nearest mountain to a place where we can suddenly see the invisible landscapes we've walked upon all along. Or maybe we are called to bear witness to an ocean sunrise, to sea gulls screaming like they did at the creation, as the sandpipers desperately search for something.

We can poke in antique shops and imagine what secrets the artifacts keep. They are not just the fossils of an earlier time. Every one of them belonged to someone once, and meant something. Their stories would be personal and intimate and would remind us that our lives are limited and enduring too.

You can go the mall or town square or bus depot and hug forty strangers. Or 100. Or 300. And while you are in the station, buy a ticket to some unknown place and ride all night listening to what the strangers say. Our lives are so very different from one another. And yet so much is the same.

And if you meditate in a snowy park at dawn, I promise, the birds will greet you with song.

There are so many other ways to press against the limits of your world. There is no need to travel half way around the globe. There are wondrous adventures half-way around the block. Our lives are not measured by the number of frequent flyer miles, stamps in our passports or world wonders seen. But the richness of our lives, its quality and its depth, is enhanced by the number and reach of our disrupted assumptions.[87]

And as you do go about reintroducing yourself to the world, if you can, do it with a friend. Something special happens when we involve people, meet them where they live and touch those things most precious, personal and essential to their lives.

Joseph Campbell said that people don't want a meaning in life, they want a *feeling* of being alive. This, by itself, seems incomplete. But it does touch other truths that are also incomplete. We all want meaning and joy. Each of us longs for our lives to be significant in some way. And as we go about seeking independence and connection, we want to be loved - loved for who we are in our own unique and messy lives.

Sometimes what speaks to us the most directly and intimately is something that makes us feel awake and alive. If your life is already howling and wonderful, filled with decency and meaning, it is so easy to get lulled to sleep by our everyday, normal routine. Or if your life is as hard and sad as a life can be, there is still a need and the space for essential joy. Microadventures allow us to re-tilt the earth so we remain fresh in our lives. They are an opportunity to respond to the question, "how do we want to live in the world?".

I want you to fall deeply in love with life; to recognize all the wonder and magic and mystery the world has to offer. I want you to know joy, and to make time to connect and to play.

Endgame

I am intrigued by chess. I don't understand it. My rank, if I had one, would fall somewhere between hack and tender beginner. I am regularly beaten by third graders who only play in aftercare with milk and cookies as they wait for their mothers to pick them up from school. Yet despite this, I am entranced by the game. That game of kings. That game upon which knights have wagered their souls for a chance to out maneuver Death[88]. On her honeymoon, Madame Dechamp had to glue the pieces to the board to stop the bridegroom from contemplating the moves of an impotent king.[89]

With its restricted movements and forced limitations, the game is maddening, infuriating. There is the odd hooking motion of the knight. The xenophobic bishops who refuse to touch a square of another color. The pawns, simpletons left over from some Samuel Beckett play, interfering with every move I want to make. Even when they are my own, they get in the way of my more free-flowing and graceful pieces, the pieces that I am when I am my best.

Yet despite the rules and limits, despite the challenges and difficulties, chess shows us life as unimaginable possibility. The number of legal chess positions is 10^{40}. The number of different possible games is 10^{120}. There are 988 million positions that can be reached after just four moves. A player thinking eight moves ahead is presented with as many possible games as there are stars in the galaxy.

Back in our usual galaxy, we're presented with evidence of a new leak in the roof. During the long commute, reckless strangers drive too fast, the irresponsible ones drive too slow. Bosses move as mute and graceless as a pawn, but are just as demanding. The dog peed on the hardwoods again.

Somehow we get lucky and stumble into an unexpected windfall that will help with the bills and the burdens and the bills. But then somewhere out in the yard, an unseen pipe bursts. Or one of the kids tumbles out of bed and a collar bone must be reset.

And when offered this Queen's Gambit, I just want to breathe. There is no time to write or pursue dreams minted when we were still young and minting dreams. The brushes are all dried in a coffee can. The portrait in the study has been unfinished for years. Time and time again when faced with that stagnant Sicilian Defense that has persistently interrupted my flow for twenty years, it seems easier to just tip the king over on its side and resign. To lay in a fetal repose and dream that everything could just stop.

And yet even with the unrepaired repairs, the debts and inequities, the heavy disappointments, our lives offer as many hopes as there are stars in the galaxy or moves on the board. In spite of our every "must do", because of our every "must do", there is so much more beauty and meaning in our lives. The difficulties that stare us in the face and say "that piece cannot be moved[90]" force us to do something new. They force us to be creative and alive and choose a brighter future, more luminous and untouched. When a poet with his borderless blank page restricts himself to some arbitrary form, *A after B after A*, he is forced to abandon the easy and cliché, and free to express something true, honest, fresh.

Our lives are worth something because they are limited.[91] Our lives have more value because they are hard. Obligations, setbacks and a greedy Queen, all ask us to be more authentic, more limitless, more beautiful. When we play, we reveal ourselves. When we play, we reveal the truest professions of the heart.[92]

The Beautiful Game

It has all come down to this. Life will give you anything and everything. Every joy and disappointment. All the tragedies and losses. It is guaranteed: You are assured unlikely miracles. And as if sitting beneath the banyan tree, or laying upon a tweed couch telling misremembered tales of childhood, we are left to try to separate "what is" from "what is useful" from "what is only belief". The simple truth is that we can savor every joy, intimately and deeply, feel every disappointment, wholly and honestly, and forever take refuge in the fact that there is never any reason for dread or despair.

As it is with any truth, this brings with it bad news. Bad because it is hard. Hard because it involves breaking reactionary habits and routines. The routines of apathy and fear, short-sightedness and self-doubt. It means letting go of the beautiful contentment that served us so well, the satisfaction, and at times even, the joy. Often it requires vision. Other times, just walking as far as we can see. And all the while it demands that sustained, consistent action that seems to contradict the very wisdom we need of knowing when to just sit still.

As it is with any truth, this brings with it good news. Good because it is easy. You already know everything you need to know. If you have ever lived a single day, you have already done everything you need now to navigate life beautifully and gracefully. It is as simple as play.

Two things, separated by time, brought all of this into focus.

The first was in 2006 watching the soccer World Cup. Brazil was one if the favorites. They usually were. The defending champions had won *A Copa do Mundo* two of the last three times and was runner up in the third. Historically, the Brazilian side was known for their particularly beautiful style of play. It was glamorous, flowing, dynamic. Defenders swirling around them, the ghosts of *A Selecao*-past, Pelé, Garrincha, Zico, Jairzinho swayed like a samba. They were creative, took risks, made unexpected passes and rejoiced in unimagined opportunities. Despite the pressure, despite the national expectations, they were relaxed and playful and the fans called it "Jogo Bonitio" the beautiful game.[93]

Yet 2006 was different. Brazil's coach had adopted a more defensive, conservative approach. This can be highly effective. Several teams have won the World Cup and league titles with this *Catenaccio* style. So as Brazil advanced through the qualifying stages and early rounds, the fans complained: "Sure they are winning, but where is the beautiful game."[94]

I didn't really understand this. I am pragmatic, American. The object of the game is to win. The team was doing just that. Where was the cause for complaint?

Then one night everything came into focus.

I have never liked board games. Whims of dice telling me whether I may advance, or to having to look someone in the eye as they point to my token and say, "that piece cannot be moved." I get too competitive and uptight. Stressed that I am going to make a mistake.

It was early in our marriage and knowing this about me, my wife did what anyone who loves you would. She ignored my protests, pushed me outside my comfort zone, and signed us up for a "couples' game night". Once a month we would get together with other families and play board games hour after hour for the entire evening.

So one night we were out with the other families playing some game, I don't remember which. My wife was not really paying attention to either the rules or what was happening on the board. She just talked and talked and absently moved her pieces around the square and made some egregious error. My tension and stress began to rise, but then I noticed something. When she realized her mistake, she started to laugh. And she laughed and she laughed and she laughed. The laughter became contagious and everyone in the room started to laugh.

It didn't matter what was happening on the board. We would go home that night and wake up the next day as if Brahman had blinked on his lotus flower, and no one would care or remember who won or lost or misplayed their cards.

What did matter, what did bind people together and ripple through to the next morning and day and every birth thereafter, was the way in which she'd played. She brought to the game everything that was honest and true and best about who she was. All the humor and affection, the passion and compassion.

The beautiful game is not about soccer, or board games or any singular, transitory event. We can go to the right schools, delay gratification, take informed guesses and follow the prescriptions of our mothers and our mother's mothers. But whether it is fate or chance or God or some other bedeviling thing, there is so much about the world that is unexpected and uncontrollable. The dishwasher will break. So will your heart. Roaches and mice will find your home comfortable and welcoming. The children you thought were safe and prepared and protected will face the same fickle world as you. And in the morning you will awake again to a meadowlark singing, as if we were still in Eden.

Think back and find those times that you were your best, the most honest and true. This is not about making things up or trying to live some imaginary life that never happened. This is about who you are, when you are, in your best moments. When you can find in "the scent of these armpits, an aroma finer than prayer."[95] Find it again and again. Regardless of what the world offers, we can always approach it with skill, heart, honor, passion and joy. The world is a game of muscle and finesse, subtlety and directedness, and we have done it all before. Life becomes meaningful by the way we play. Play it beautifully.[96][97]

God and Intimacy

"Tell me what you do with the food you eat, and I'll tell you who you are. Some turn their food into fat and manure, some into work and good humor, and others, I'm told, into God." - Nikos Kazantzakis, Zorba the Greek

Somewhere in the middle of awkward adolescence, I wandered to the church each week with other muddled teens for lessons on the faith of our tribe. It was an older school girl who taught the class with its tenets and catechisms.

As the other kids fidgeted and doodled, or tossed chalk and crumpled paper, I sat in the front row asking questions. Our teacher would speak about what it means to live in this world, and how to make sense of things. There was so much I wanted to understand and needed to know. So I asked, and listened, and asked again, those questions that no one could possibly answer.

When the date of our initiation came, all of the novitiates were gathered in the front of the church with the attendant priest and altar boys. Our teacher had arranged that we would perform a play for the congregation. One of the paper crumplers would be our Savior. The

Lord's mother, her sister, and all the other Mary's were there. I, the one who asked about that which resides in hearts of men, was given the role of Pilate, and told to slap Jesus upon the altar.

Whenever I meet someone who says they do not believe in God, I ask them to describe the deity they have come to reject. I usually cannot believe in that God either. But whenever I meet someone who does claim faith, the conversation is typically harder. At times, there is a zealous certainty. At times it is more subtle and nuanced. "God" can mean so many things.

First there was *God-the-Dogmatic,* anthropomorphic and thick with tradition. So punctuated with holy absolutes there is no room for metaphors. He is the *"God of Abraham, Isaac and Jacob"*[98] found in every faith. Somehow, I could never tether my hope to anything so clear and constant, this promise of something to count on.

Then came *God-the-Construct,* conceived in cortical ecstasy by philosophers and other apologists: beautiful; esoteric; as finely crafted as the universe. But *He* was more Distance than Humanity. This sort of god lacked the instructive feel of what it means to live a human life.

Speak to me of personal struggle. Speak to me of how you've discovered deep beauty in the crass and quotidian. With your eyes, tell me about your heart-felt *longing* for answers to questions that cannot be answered with the words to which we've grown accustomed. It does not matter if the struggle yields anything that you can, in good faith, call "god". That full, four-chambered beating you feel in the center of your chest proves the struggle has been worth it all along.

The God I understand is discussions with old men, their wrinkles the signs of honor for the hardships they've endured. It is the silent steadfastness of teenage girls trying to navigate a world full of pettiness and cruelty that reasons will never justify. It is barefooted boys chasing pigeons in the park and the sweetness of berries and apples that always return, miraculously, season after season. Speak to me of metaphors and of metaphorical truths. Speak to me of an ethic that errs on the side of forgiveness and gratitude, and is expressed as humility and unbridled compassion. Rather than get stuck with notions of what a god is or might be, speak to me of a sacredness in life that is more dependent on intimate questions than on any comprehensible answer.

One might ask, "*Isn't there a contradiction between what people do and their stated beliefs?*".

Of course.

Deliver us from the temptation to ascribe duplicity only to strangers and our brothers-in-law. Every one of us is twin to an afterbirth. No one of us can claim immunity from the appearance of hypocrisy. It is just that when we deviate from the laws we covet, we understand our reasons.[99] We have read the nuanced exceptions in our personal constitution, and can, in good faith, justify the actions that others cannot hope to understand.

Rather than seek nourishment in belief as tasteless as the white of an egg,[100] what if we acted in accordance with what the Prophets say: Jesus and Mohammad; Buddha and Krishna; Black Elk and Mandela; Martin Luther King? What if we became a *refuge for human kind?*[101] If we loved our enemies, especially when they were cruel or unreasonable, arrogant and ignorant and insisting on the last scream. What if we had the strength and wisdom and mercy to free them from their anger when they spat upon us or broke our fingers?[102] Because in our better moments, we do have that strength and wisdom and mercy.

How would we behave differently if we believed we were the bodhisattva of compassion come back? What if we acted as if whoever saves a single life saves the whole world?[103] What if we humbled ourselves like children[104], or in the middle of an argument, took a child and sat him or her down in between us and embraced? How would that change the debates in the Congress and in the courts?

Let us breathe life into the metaphors. Let us look upon every tradition and every faith groping for truth as an effort to make personal the golden rule. What if we stopped worrying about whether there is a god, or who believes in which, or if the "other" is godless or descended from apes, and instead saw kindness as *the mark of faith?*[105] Forget about belief for a while. What if we acted as if angels and gods were real? That no angel would ever descend in a place where we allowed even on one person to remain hungry?[106] What if we acted as if the gods changed shape and came back as beggars and prostitutes and widows?[107] What if we looked eye-to-eye with every stranger, every friend, with the family member toward whom we feel contempt, and embraced the divine in them with all that is human and weak and radiant in ourselves? We truly are a mix of mud and dreams, and all the while, we are better than we thought we were. Let us live our lives as if we were in love with the world. *"Dear children, let us not love with words or tongue but with actions and in truth."*[108]

It is hard. We are so rushed and hurried and busied that we risk losing that which is the most essential to our humanity. Martin Buber warned that in our haste, in the midst of all of our wonderful progress, we would lose the ability to enter into those intimate I-Thou relationships that make us the most human.[109] Milosz sought to recover a reverence for being.[110] Walcott lamented that awe has been lost to our time.[111] The "god" that once sustained us has become *God-the-Mundane*, cliché and empty, and as impotent as a concept.

It is hard. Everything we need and desire, converge: A safe neighborhood; good schools; healthy foods; expressions of culture; a little leisure; and some entertainment at the end of the week. So like a sacrifice upon the alter, I exchange time and life energy for a desk job in an unmarked room. In my less than lucid moments, I think of abandoning everything, joining an ashram or monastery, and focusing fully and completely on matters of the spirit. For if the most beautiful things they say about the gods were true, how could we not give up everything in absolute devotion? But we cannot simply cast off everything, cannot just run away. Spiritual retreat would mean the loss of something more substantial the just the hum of iridescent office lights.

It is hard. This world, our world, is measured by its entropy: the level of disorder that forever increases with time. Left alone, things fall apart: Leaves let loose from the trees. Sidewalks crack and fill with weeds. Chaos, disorder, hunger, suffering, inequity, injustice, crass indignities and indiscretions and every other pestilence that Pandora loosed upon the world will happen, and they happen mindlessly.

Enter upon the stage some small, strutting biped, limited by time and imagination and haunted by both illusions of grandeur and feelings of inadequacy. We can restore some of that order and connect the seemingly desperate things. We are the ones who give names to every creature. We pull weeds from the garden and prune the apple tree. The simple truth is the holiest of temples has no walls. There are Buddhas all around us, fixing a leaky pipe or interpreting a spreadsheet in the next cubical. Every one of our neighbors needs a Samaritan to find and touch them where they lay, and angels are the helpers that appear everywhere.

Live intimately. Doing so opens us to our connections with the world. Wolves were released into Yellowstone and the birds returned and the banks of the rivers became firm.[112] The "fecal blooms" of whales fertilize plant plankton, making food for fish and krill and absorbing carbon from air allowing us to breathe. We are a part of this nature too. The rhythm of our heart beat, the pulse of our breath, the flow of our blood, all share coherence with the stars and the tides and the winds. As I inhale, exhale and exchange breath with friends and those I thought were not friends, I take into to my lungs those same particles that have circulated the globe since the first dawn. As I breathe out I expel something to share with my children, and my children's children's children.

When we walk upon the earth, gentle and aware, with beauty and grace, we connect back into our bodies. Holiness is there in the way we eat and breathe and bathe. It is in every movement and motion. It is there waiting for us to slip an arm through a shirt sleeve or to rise up from a chair and walk across the room. Holiness is looking for us in those moments when we are tempted to linger: waiting in line at the DMV; sitting in traffic; or accidently treating the whole of our lives as nothing more than a pastime on the way to death. When we connect to the small intimate acts of living, we become the drop merging into the sea, that in return, feels a whole ocean merging back.[113]

This felt-awareness swaddles and wraps us and makes us small and secure. Every care-fear-concern-trouble-pain somehow becomes less onerous and less oppressive. It is as if by some trick, this awareness of our minuscule-momentary lives lifts us upon an arc of importance and secures for us an essential place in the horizon. The middle-aged woman jogging around the park in sweat pants and out of breath is just as vital to this landscape as are the foaming dogwoods and flowering azaleas, an invisible thrush and pollen-drunk bee. When we pay attention, every paradox of the world reveals itself and we realize there is no paradox. There is no such thing as irony. The disparate, nonsensical shapes of this puzzle all fit together perfectly and provide something firm. The almond tree roots to the universe and blossoms. When we root to the universe, we blossom.

There is a job for us upon this earth. If we hope to flourish, thrive and live our lives with happiness, meaning and import, we must accept chaos and decline as a natural, undiscriminating part of the world. So too must we take deliberate, patient action to bring some small order in our little corner of time. God, if there were one, would need us, the dung beetles of the earth, to make the world better.[114]

Sacredness is felt and shared. All of life becomes holy when we make ourselves patiently aware, when we slow down and ease into the gratitude and gracefulness that is possible for us. All of life becomes holy when we accept, with or without contentment, the linear and the inexplicable, and when we become vitally and intimately engaged with all that is essential and mundane, for everything is essential and mundane. It is about inserting more humanity into every interaction. It is about going about the world with beauty, honor and grace, and living life as though it were a beautiful game. Every act of our lives, every breath, points to something more, something beyond itself. We are the intimate. Every act makes us the metaphor that explains everything.

Living Will

Someday I will decline.[115] My gray matter will become grayer still. My wits and memories will grow threadbare and worn thin. The people I loved, and those who loved me, will come to my cell with their hopes and shimmering reminiscences only to find that they have become strangers to this clod of earth.

Please do not be saddened. The memories did what they were supposed to do. The glorious futures that glimmered out on the horizon have all come and all passed.

But there is tender business still, beyond all faculty and recall.

Take my hand. Or hook your arm around my waist while cupping my elbow to steady me. Help me to find the beautiful things: Birds that sing under the cover of summer; the helping women with their rolled up sleeves; and down by the pond there are those spiders who walk upon water and the incarnation is proved.

Point me to where the laughter comes from, to the barefooted boys in the grass and their dark-haired sisters in bright dresses. Bring me flowers, or leaves of linden and sassafras. Their green-stemmed fragrance is all the permanence I need.

Show me everything you find sweet and miraculous. We are no longer limited by our memories and our dreams.

And if my eyes or ears have failed, speak to me in some other language. Help me to see or feel or hear why the willows sway as they are fed by something they cannot see. Introduce me to the sun's rays again. Remind me of my every inhalation and exhalation in this moment. For as long as we have breath, there is no need for that other heaven.

* * * * *

"It is sweet to think I was a companion in an expedition that never ends" — Czesław Miłosz

Afterword: A Reader's Guide

Poet and author Jorge Luis Borges said that "*A book is not an isolated being, it is a relationship, an axis of innumerable relationships.*" Some books are polite conversations with strangers while we await an appointment or a cross-town bus. Friendly. Pleasant enough. A well-wishing while passing the time, without having to inconvenience ourselves.

Others however, are more all-encompassing: They transform and transmit us in lasting ways, leaving us better than we were before. This transmutative power of books is not limited to the great works of literature. There can be moments in any *encounter* that touch something deeper and more fundamental within us. Sitting in silence, the author offers one side of a script for a meeting between strangers that might never happen. Every now and then, something in the reader comes out, a thought or history or dream, and greets the words where they were left. It becomes an intimate dialogue, personal and universal.

Every author hopes to play a part in this sacred consultation. If I could, I would sit down with each and every one of you, look you in the eyes, and point to all the beauty and majesty in your lives! I want you to know that *you are better than you thought you were, stronger and more gentle and capable of infinitely more. You have the power to make other people's lives better and more hopeful and meaningful.* But how can I convince you of this, when I am limited to only words on a page!

And so, in my one last, resolute attempt, I offer you the following thoughts and threads and questions. As you read *Mud and Dreams*, use these "*Exercises in Humanity*" to explore what it means for you to be human, with everything that entails: all the hopes and joys, each challenge and desperate disappointment.

My hope is that you will come back to this book again and again. You are changing, after all. And "Life" is continually intervening and offering you new destinies (whether you like them or not) and taking things away. If you come back and read these essays again, they might just ask new questions under the change in circumstance, and you will discover all over again that *your life is worth more than you imaged.*

As you read *Mud and Dreams* and explore the questions below, *who are the other people that come to mind?* Share your thoughts with them. Tell them what you want for their lives. I cannot sit down with each one of you, **but you can with them.** Look your loved ones and friends in the eyes. Renew your vows to one another and go through these essays and exercises together. Let *Mud and Dreams* become an *axis of innumerable relationships;* connecting what is quiet and beautiful in you, with everything that is shared and different, sacred and wonderful within them.

Exercises in Humanity

PART I. LIVING IN THE WORLD

Sinkholes

In "Sinkholes", "flourishing" is described as that experience of being "wholly alive" and "intimately engaged" in life and being able to "fully participate in all aspects of being human." That would require us to open ourselves to everything, to allow ourselves to be vulnerable and to risk heartache, disappointment and pain.

1) How often do you allow yourself to let go and be open in this way? In which domains are you the most open? In which are you more guarded?

2) When things are difficult, sometimes it is easier and feels better, to simply cut ourselves off, to be stoic and not allow ourselves feel. How do you balance vulnerability and stoicism?

3) What are you willing to do today to allow yourself to be open to risk and pain?

Horizons

Everything we experience and perceive points past itself to a world beyond awareness, one comprised of anticipation, hope and expectation. This is true of physical experiences. But so too does it impact our cultural, psychosocial, and other experiences of ourselves and of the world.

1) An Exercise: Pick one of your personal horizons. Maybe it is the visual bubble around you. Maybe it is the auditory.
   a) Block out all other sensations. Focus upon what is within your direct experience. Linger there and just notice. What limits do you bump up against?
   b) Now, imagine what lies just beyond those limits. What assumptions are you making? What new worlds open up for you? What possibilities are there?

2) Horizons are about assumptions. They mark the boundaries between what we know and what we expect about our physical, cultural, social and other worlds. Think about something important in your life that troubles you. You bring to that moment certain facts about the past or future or present. Maybe your assumptions are tethered to a history that might no longer be true or relevant or useful. What other facts could offer a different story? One of hope or courage, forgiveness or even joy?

3) We tell ourselves stories every day that are absolutely true. They protect us, validate us, and draw others to our side. What is your story? Is this one that you would choose for your life? Considering the same "facts", are there other conclusions you can draw that allow you to see you are better than you thought you were, stronger, more kind, more capable of forgiveness and love?

The Great White

As we saw in "Horizons", everything we experience and perceive points past itself to a world comprised of anticipation, hope and expectation. Our thoughts about things, experiences, events are different than the things themselves. Different in meaningful ways. Sometimes it is the thought that is more real, more impactful and more meaningful then the fact or event. Thoughts can increase our blood pressure, causes gastro-intestinal problems, hinder our immune systems and have other tangible, measurable effects. This does not mean that there is no such thing as truth, or that truth is relative. Rather, it is just that there are multiple, credible interpretations of the events of our world.

1) Think about a time that your thoughts about something had a bigger, stronger influence on you, than the thing itself. What was going on? What were the effects? (Physical? Psychological? Social?) What other options were available to you? What would have been the effect to your happiness, effectiveness or well-being if you have pursued a different option?

2) How would you have responded to the shark in *The Great White*? Is that how you tend to react to life events? How does your response to the shark help you in life? How does it interfere with your happiness, effectiveness or well-being?

3) What would you have to do to allow yourself to be flexible in your appraisals the world (e.g. sometimes a shark is a just a shark, sometimes it is a threat, and often it is something to celebrate.) How would that empower you? What freedoms would that create?

Bad Breath

Beauty can be found in the most unexpected places. The poet Pablo Neruda sought, "a poetry impure as the clothing we wear, or our bodies, soup-stained, soiled with our shameful behavior, our wrinkles and vigils and dreams . . . ". Walt Whitman, a "pragmatist aesthetic", saw everything as holy and a miracle. As set out "Bad Breath", Beauty, and a deeper connection to all of humanity, might even be found in the sour, unbrushed breath of a stranger.

1) Tell about a time you found something "beautiful" in the crass, foul or dirty? What was going on then? What was it about that moment that allowed you to see something resembling beauty in what you would have thought was profane?

2) What would happen if you looked for the beautiful, or the positive and life affirming, in the things that usually provoke disgust in you?

3) An Exercise: Today, look for the beauty that is all around you. Extra Credit: Find what is life affirming and miraculous in the dingy, crass or imperfect. Share the experience with a friend. (Repeat as often as possible.)

Changing the Narrative

The stories we tell ourselves about our lives matter. The things we say to others about them and their lives matters too. So often, the stories we tell are simply one interpretation, based on one set of facts. There may be other stories and other facts that are more useful and with a deeper truth.

1) Tell about a time you have been a victim. How is that continuing to affect you? Without denying the pain, how has it benefited you? In what ways has it held you back?

2) What other evidence do you have that maybe you are stronger than you thought? More in control and capable? More awe inspiring?

3) Think back to a time when someone did something, offered you a kindness, or treated you in some manner, that changed you. Who was it? What did they do or say? In what ways did it change how you saw yourself? In what ways can you have a similar positive effect on others?

PART II. BEING TOWARD OTHERS

Refuge in Love

In the face of hardship, injustice or the coldest of traumas, the only answer is to hold even tighter to kindness and to care even more deeply. If we interrupt the violence and insert humanity into inhuman situations, that goodness, kindness, and love will also spread. We might not be immediately aware of how or why, but when we increase the humility, compassion, understanding, vulnerability, kindness or love, somewhere it will heal and build.

1) Tell about a time when someone showed you love or deep kindness or understanding when you did not expect it?

2) Think of someone who has does something to you that you are having a hard time forgiving. What would you have to let go of to commit to love and kindness in this circumstance?

3) What is one thing you can do today to insert more love and kindness into the world? Who can help you keep this commitment?

Hugging the Horse's Head

Life is hard. It is not fair. It is filled with rapturous beautiful moments and it all ends much, much too quickly. Too often, too many people are unnecessarily cruel, or mindless, or oblivious to inequities. Hugging the Horse's Head proposes a remedy.

1) What do you do to keep from losing hope when others are unkind?

2) Who are your models: Who can you count on to always stand up for kindness and respect? Who brings the best of humanity out of you?

3) What can we do to nurture a culture of kindness and respect? What can you do personally? Who else can you recruit that would commit to kindness?

What Ever Happened to Conner MacBride

Sometimes the angels that appear in our lives, do so in surprising and unexpected ways.

1) Who are the people you can count on? What can you do today to foster and nurture those relationships? What can you do today to cultivate deeper relationships with others?

2) Sometimes it is our closest friends who let us down. And yet they are there for us in so many other ways. Forgive them. Are there times you may have let someone dear to you down, or pressured them, without even realizing it? Forgive yourself and reach out to them.

3) What can we do to encourage people to take care of one another?

Absence and Return

You are better than you think you are. You can overcome tremendous hardships and challenges. And your life matters in ways you might never suspect. And yet, we are all part of something bigger; a more intricate fabric. The infinite, innumerable people around you are just as miraculous and wonderful and worthy of awe. The way we encounter one another – how we listen, how we respond, whether we touch – matters.

1) Humility often gets tangled up with a sense of low self-regard or unworthiness. It can become a form of self-abuse (*humiliate*) rather than a sense of groundedness (*humus*, of the earth). What can you do to maintain your sense of worth and specialness, while also remaining grounded?

2) An Exercise. How comfortable are you with quiet success? The next time you achieve something, look for the role others played (We rarely do it alone). Publicly acknowledge them.

3) An Exercise. Today, look for the miraculous in another person. Allow yourself to feel a sense of respect and awe, without feeling competitive or envy, jealousy or self-reproach.

The Sacred Thread

Lovely, inexpensive and discrete, it only takes a ring on our little finger, a label pin, or a simple colored string tied around the wrist to serve as an "anchor" for our well-being, a reminder of whatever we have infused into that talisman. "The Sacred Thread" traces a symbol of connection, protection and kindness through the collective unconscious of many cultures. Not only does this common symbol across time and culture remind us of the best aspects of human nature, but it also serves to link each of us together, across time and space, tying us to our shared humanity.

1) What symbol or rituals can you use or create to sustain you? What virtue or reminder would you "infuse" into this practice?

What can you do to keep this practice fresh, to avoid the dulling of habit and allow your anchor or practice to continue to silently nourish you?

2) Are there others that you will share your practice or symbol with? Who can you draw into your circle? Who else can you touch?

3) If you were going to do one thing today to enhance the bonds or bridges with the others in your life, what would you do? Go ahead. Give yourself that gift.

Throwing Bullets in the Fire

From time-to-time, every one of us does thoughtless or foolish things. However as long as nothing goes wrong, they are easy to forget. We might even look back at them with warm memories or laugh. Yet when we read in the paper about something that went horribly wrong after someone did something mindless or stupid, it is easy to criticize or blame. Every one of us is negligent. But to be negligent and unlucky? That is a crime no one can ever shake off.

1) Think of some accident or negligent trauma in the public consciousness. Now think of something foolish or mindless that you have done, that could have gone seriously wrong? How does that inform how you think about the public trauma?

2) What can you offer in the face of these tragedies? To the person who caused it? To their family? To the families of the affected? To your own family? To the community?

3) What can you do today to increase kindness or understanding or patience in the community or public dialog? Looking at the world around you, what gives you hope?

PART III. OVERCOMING AND ACCEPTANCE

Lost at Sea

In its survival training, the US Air Force teaches the Rule of Three. It includes in part, that one cannot live more than three weeks without food, three days without water or three minutes without air. Equally important, we cannot survive more than three seconds without spirit or hope. People who have hope are more successful in almost every domain n life: they live longer, have better relationships, and have more success at work. In addition, in study-after-study, across cultures, hope is one of a handful of strengths most connected with happiness.

1) What long range or difficult dream are you are pursuing? Or what hardship has life shoved in your face that has you fighting to overcome or struggling to just hang on? What keeps you going?

2) While circumstances will not always go as we like, there are things around us every day upon which to our hope. If you allow yourself to see them, there are always resources and tools and unexpected opportunities. Yet a hopeful wishing can also lead us to overlook the potholes and difficulties that will also occur. What can you do to maintain the clarity to see the hard facts as they are, and yet remain attentive to the things you can do?

3) What can you do to inspire hope in others?

It Is Not the Mountain We Conquer

When pursuing any goal, we balance our expected likelihood of success, against the things we must sacrifice. But it is the value we place in it, our many "why's", that act as a powerful driver toward that goal.

1) What is one of you big, life goals? What dream or a challenge you are striving toward? What does the dream-goal say about you?

2) While in pursuit, you will have to give up a lot. Often we must decline good things, things that can give us happiness. And while I the middle of pursuing a dream, you will encounter setbacks and doubts that cause you to question your own self-worth. Well-meaning loved ones will even encourage you to accept something less. What are your two or three biggest "why's" - the ones most central to who you are?

3) What would happen if you achieved this dream? How would you see yourself differently? What would happen if you failed to reach your goal?

To Repair with Gold

It might come as a surprise, but people do grow in the wake of trauma. It is not inevitable. It does not mean you wouldn't trade whatever benefits you received, if you could have avoided the pain. But more often than not, when things go wrong, most people do not dry up, crumble and fall to pieces. You are better than you think you are. Stronger. More adaptive. You are not without reasons for hope or meaning or love, even when faced with even the deepest traumas. You can find joy again.

1) Are there any hardships you have faced that seem insurmountable, or that you are not sure that you can recover from? Without taking away from the truth of your pain:
   a. Were there any opportunities that emerged? Possibilities that you may not have noticed or that were not present before?
   b. Has your relationship with anyone changed for the better because of the crisis? Who? Who are some other people to whom you could draw closer?
   c. In what ways did you discover you are stronger and more capable than you imagined?
   d. If you are religious, are there ways in which the crisis has deepened your faith?
   e. Are there ways in which the trauma gave you a greater appreciation for life?

145

2) So often, trauma disrupts our most fundamental beliefs about the world – the very things upon which we depended. What can you do to realign your beliefs so you accept the truths of the trauma, *and yet* give you a greater sense of love for the world? What can you do to accept the brokenness as part of your history, *and yet* see yourself as stronger and more beautiful, precisely because of where things had been broken.

3) What can you do to give others hope?

Learning to Ride a Bicycle

One of the hardest truths we have to face in life, is that we cannot always protect the ones we love from the hardships, misfortunates and tragedies that will confront them.

1) Think about someone you love. If some god or goddess offered to come down and write every detail of his or her life on their forehead in advance, would you accept? Why or why not?

2) It is too easy to get so caught up in the everyday must-dos and should-dos that we are not as caring, patient or centered as we would like with the ones we love. Sometimes we are too hard on ourselves about not being as caring, patient or centered. What can you do to forgive yourself? Tell about a time that you were your most caring when it could have been easy not too. What can you do to remind yourself to give the best of who you are to the ones you love?

3) Who brings the best out of you? Thank them.

Sardines

"Sardines" builds upon the theme from "Learning to Ride a Bicycle", that we cannot protect the ones we love from the hardships they will face. But while that essay looked at the things we can do when life is out of control, Sardines, asks us to accept what we cannot know and continue to thrive anyway.

1) Think for a moment about something difficult or unfair that you don't understand. To accept, move forward and even to flourish, does not mean ignoring whatever happened. It does not mean betraying or minimizing our suffering. What would it take for you to continue to move forward, flourish and find joy, even if you never understand "why" the bad thing happened?

2) Recognizing that you might never know "why", what would you need to find your center and strength?

3) Who would you like to be able to turn toward for support? What can you do today to build those nurturing relationships?

The Exquisite Tapestry

We are so caught up in the everyday-overwhelming, we often take for granted the good things in our lives. It is even easier, to fail to see the hidden treasures that the hardships can sometimes bring. However, what may be the hardest and most rewarding and nourishing of all, is moving beyond acceptance (Learning to Ride a Bicycle; Sardines) and growth (To Repair With Gold) and letting ourselves feel grateful that we are simply a part of it all.

1) Today, look around you and notice three things you feel grateful for. What role did you play in having them occur in your life? (Repeat, often)

2) When moments or the events of life are hard, what are the things you can find solace in?

3) How would it feel if you could envelop all of the hard things and disappointments in life into an all-encompassing gratefulness that is not dependent upon any benefits the hardships might have brought? What would you need to let yourself do this?

PART IV. EMBRACING IT ALL

Earthworms and Puddles

Great joy and contentment can often come from simply slowing down and savoring the big or little thigs life has to offer.

1) How easy is it for you to slow down? What does it look like for you?

2) What can you take to remind yourself to slow down?

3) An Exercise: Select something to savor today. It could be a good meal, a piece of music or literature, time with a friend, the movement of your body, or a single grape. It is up to you. Go out and enjoy this thing or activity as fully and deeply as you can.

Secret Destinations

All of us have certain psychological and physical needs. Some are common and shared across the human race. Others are local and specific and personal to who we are. Perhaps one of the best things we can do for our health and happiness, our effectiveness and well-being, is to practice letting go of precisely those things we need.

1) When is the last time you deliberately set out to put yourself off balance? What did you do? If you have not tried it, what can you do?

2) What would you need to do, to allow yourself to laugh in those moments when you did not have those things you thought were fundamental, the things you thought you needed? What would you need to do, to allow yourself to continue to be happy and to flourish?

3) *Secret Destinations* proposes putting yourself off-balance through making travel difficult. What are some other ways you can deliberately put yourself off balance?

Adventures Just Outside Your Door

The last essay, looked at using "Travel" to deliberately challenge our assumptions and sense of need. However, opportunities for "adventure" are all around us. Simple, inexpensive, if we are attentive and aware, even a short walk around the corner can open a whole new world of disrupted expectations. We can put ourselves off balance again so that we might regain our equilibrium and recover a sense of zest and wonder in our lives.

1) Some microadventures will require you to stretch and push yourself. Others can be smaller, yet still allow you to experience your world and expectations differently. What are some "easy" microadventures you can do right away? Which of your friends can come with you?

2) Which ideas are a little bigger, that both scare and excite you?

3) Pick at least one idea from your lists above with your friend and mark it on your calendar.

Endgame

One does not have to be skilled at chess, or understand the rules of poetry, to recognize the paradoxical truths they present: It is limitations and restrictions, that provide the freedom and urgency to living. At the end of a chess match, or in the middle of a life, when the beautiful symmetry of the beginning is gone, life reduced to its essentials, and we are called upon to act. This is true of the losses <u>in</u> life and this is true of the loss <u>of</u> life - our own, and of our loved ones. The difficulties and definitive end point, provide a meaning and context to our lives, that can free us and make our time here beautiful and filled with meaning.

1) Think about some loss or trouble you have had or are currently going through. What would it take for you to see that difficulty as setting you free, or providing even greater meaning in your life?

2) How would it feel differently if in the face of this trouble, you opened yourself and stepped forward into your freedom? What would that look like? What would you have to let go of to do so?

3) What kind of person do your troubles make you? How do you feel about that? What can you do to find a different way of being in the face of the troubles?

The Beautiful Game

Play is good for us. It adds a freshness and puts the life back into life. However, the hard facts of the world do not always invite us to celebrate. Yet no matter how inconvenient, hard or tragic life can be, we always have the chance to bring to it all of our heart and joy, creativity and humility. No matter what fate hands us, we can live our lives beautifully. This will not take away our troubles. The necessities we are given may still be brutal and harsh. Yet no matter the facts of our world, in the end, it comes down to how we want to live our lives. How we want to be in the world, and the effect we want to have on one another.

1) How easy is it for you to let yourself play? Does anything typically get in the way? What can you do to allow yourself to play more often?

2) Think about a task or obligation that you do not want to do. Maybe it is something at work or household chores. Maybe it is being attentive to your diet or exercising after a long day. How can you turn that into a game? What can you do to make it playful and genuinely enjoyable?

3) Can you allow yourself to approach your days playfully when life is hard or cruel? What would play look like in these moments? How would you be more effective? What do you need to be able to approach life with the seriousness it demands, and yet still allow yourself to play?

Of God and Intimacy

Despite hesitations and reasons for doubt, a notion of a god or gods has persisted in every culture throughout time. Sometimes it is concrete and exacting. Other times, it is more fluid. There is something sustaining in seeing ourselves connected to something beyond ourselves.

1) Regardless of whatever images of god you have been given by your church, family, culture, etc., what sort of "god" *could* you believe in? What would make that "god" personal and meaningful for you?

2) How would it change the way you lived in the world, if you went looking for this thing we are now calling "god"? How would you behave differently with others? How would you see yourself differently?

3) Thought experiment. What if we offered love to our enemies, or to those who provoke our anger or disgust? What if we were especially diligent when they were cruel, arrogant or unreasonable? How would that change you? What are you willing to do to commit to injecting increasing levels of love and kindness into the world?

A Living Will

While most of us will not become senile, it is an all too common fear. We need only watch someone else slide into someone unrecognizable, for us to fear for our own futures, or those of our loved ones. One of our great tasks in life is learning how to navigate in a world where there is so much that it outside of our control. Navigate not just the practical next steps, but how do we cultivate the ability to appreciate, embrace and even celebrate life, when so much is uncertain.

1) If you were to decline, what would you want for your loved ones? What message would you want to give them? How would you want them to care for themselves? Have you ever told them this? Is there something you can do now to express it

too them? Maybe write it down somewhere so they don't forget?

2) Where does "meaning" come from, if we have lost our memories or the other things we had counted on for meaning?

3) What are you going to leave behind? (Small things can have a big, big effect.) What can you do to ensure that the lives of your loved ones remain beautiful and worthwhile?

Acknowledgments

There is a tendency to think of writing as a solitary act: The author, alone at the keyboard, discovering what he or she knows. To a certain extent this is true. To write demands an unreasonable number of hours shutting my door to the outside world, compromising my eyes and health with all that staring and tapping in the glow of the screen.

But even though the *act* of writing is solitary, I never once was alone. There were so many people who helped and encouraged me and kept me coming back to the page when the torments of writing seemed like they were too much. I would be awake at my computer at 3:00 in the morning while my wife and children were asleep. *Doubt*, that malevolent imp, would whisper or scream in my ear that I was wasting my time and to go back to bed. "No one would ever read this anyway," the voice would say. And yet there were so many people who were there with me, invisibly, speaking with the silence of a cloud or a tree, strengthening me and kept me going.

I am grateful to so many, for so much.

First, there is my wife Jenny, and my children Andrieu, Abigail and Allison. We truly do write to discover what we know. The things in this book are what you taught me, the things we discovered together. Always remember your lives are good and beautiful and filled with hope and magic. Look for it. No matter what the world puts in your way or throws at you, fight for it. The hope and beauty will always be there waiting for you.

And to my parents, John and Nancy Doyle, and my sister, Cindy Dikeman, who have always offered me love and support.

Then there were those people with the stamina and grace to read complete drafts of the book and help keep me honest: Emily Han of Lyrical Editing (www.lyricalediting.com), author Katy Munger (https://katymunger.wordpress.com/), Aren Cohen, Greg Quinting, and Jenny again.

John Howard Moore (http://jhmoore.com) shared his vision and expertise in helping design the cover. Kemah E. P. Washington (http://brandillymc.com) crafted beautiful outreach materials. And both offered encouragement and ideas beyond that. The artist Samy Bris allowed me use his lithograph, *Shabbat* for the cover, a picture which has been hanging on my wall for twenty-five years. And Samantha Ruehl kept my frustration at bay as she calmly led me through formatting and other technical issues.

Then there were the countless people who commented on individual essays, shared them with strangers and friends, sent me private back channel messages, quoted me to myself or were generous with their praise. I can't possible list everyone.

Some of my earliest most vigilant supporters include:

Kenny Barron, Joe Bennett, Nancy Blackwell, Sulynn Choong, Jessica Doyle, Karen Garman, Deb Giffen, Geoffery Gunter, Macy Hamm, Christine Hill, Susan J. Hwang, Sandy James, Justin Landwehr, Sandy Lewis, Ellen M. Meier, Jane Needham, David O'Mahony, Jyotsna O'Mahony, David Pollay, Frank Silber, Jan Stanley, George Eman Valliant, Todd Whitmer, Ivor Whitson and Mitzi Searcy Willis.

And there were still others:

Louis Alloro, Will Andrus, Scott Asalone, Violette de Ayala, Tarek Azhari, Chase Bernard, Mandy Nicolau Bernard, Anuj Bhargava, Eric Bolash, Shannon Black-Beer, Iris Marie Bloom, Matt Botzum, Brian Brown, Dan Bowling, John Burns, Valorie Burton, Wes Camden, Derrick Carpenter, Donna Carter, Kathy Chavis, Mike Collins, Charlie Cooper, Carmen Cox, Robert Crawford, Bobbi Croy, Marge Dougherty, Dave Dulong, Paula Davis-Laack, Bright Dickson, John Eastman, John Erwin, Michael Faisst, Rasa Telenkova Fawzy, Sherri Fisher, Teresa Flores, Evan Fultz, Monica Gao, Doug Gillan, Craig Gottschalk, Kristen Cartwright Gottschalk, Can Güralp, Izzy Guzman, Margaret Hudson Greenburg, Jefferson Griffin, John Gronde, Sandi Hagopian, Kimon Haldas, Geoff Hall, Nicholas Hall, George Harder, Nick Hernandez, Dane Huffman, Hope Inge, Louisa Jewell, Ben Jorgensen, Amy Ray Jones, Bryce Kaye, Jennifer Cloyd

Konomos, Rich Konzelman, Ken Lambert, Ellen Lang, Jen Lee, Robert Mack, Mark Mahoney, Senia Maymin, Cathi Stahlnecker Mohundro, Rhett Moody, David Moreau, Masaki Nakamura, Ryan M. Niemiec, Dave Manning, Abbie Meyer Mota, Elaine O'Brien, Liisa Ogburn, Corey Palmer, Chris Petrini, David Pfeil, Radhika Punshi, Mark Ramey, Ann Wray Ramey, Lola Rokni, Jennifer Rucinski, Laura San Miguel, Amy Morgan Saul, Kirsten Street Sebek, Lisa Sansom, David Shearon, Wes Sims, Julie Snyder, Geoff Smith, Stig Magnus Soløy, Kunal Sood, Mary Santiago, Liz Desimone Savitsky, Kristen Slusar, Todd Spiering, Renee Tatum, Lionel Todd, Jennifer Katherine Peeler Truman, Kaori Uno, Fabio Velasco, Don Von Hagen, Frank Wall, Doug Ward, Brian Wilcox, Jeremy Wilson, Paul T. P. Wong, Rachael Wooten, Corey Zadik and Jason Zellner.

I cannot express enough how grateful I am to all of you.

Sean

Notes and References

Part I. Living in the World

Horizons

A version of this essay previously appeared on Positive Psychology News Daily, here: http://positivepsychologynews.com/news/sean-doyle/2013061426446 and also on the author's website at http://www.johnseandoyle.com/beyond-the-horizon/

[1] For more on Maurice Merleau-Ponty, see Flynn, Bernard, "Maurice Merleau-Ponty", The Stanford Encyclopedia of Philosophy (Fall 2011 Edition), Edward N. Zalta (ed.), http://plato.stanford.edu/archives/fall2011/entries/merleau-ponty/

[2] For more on Edmund Husserl, see Beyer, Christian, "Edmund Husserl", The Stanford Encyclopedia of Philosophy (Summer 2013 Edition), Edward N. Zalta (ed.), forthcoming URL = http://plato.stanford.edu/archives/sum2013/entries/husserl/

[3] William James frequently used his "cash-value" metaphor to assess whether an idea or a concept, in the words of Cotkin, "worked, assimilated new knowledge into one's previous stock of truths, and satisfied our desire for intellectual clarity, simplicity, and beauty." Cotkin, George. "William James and the Cash-Value Metaphor." *ETC: A Review of General Semantics*, vol. 42, no. 1, 1985, pp. 37–46. https://pdfs.semanticscholar.org/7193/d24abb7333981c49c6c1cea3d994affce67e.pdf.
For more, see also James, William. *Pragmatism: A New Name for Some Old Ways of Thinking* (1907), Hackett Publishing 1981: ISBN 0-915145-05-7, Dover 1995: ISBN 0-486-28270-8

[4] *Long have you timidly waded*
Holding a plank by the shore,
Now I will you to be a bold swimmer,
To jump off in the midst of the sea,
Rise again, nod to me, shout,
And laughingly dash with your hair.
Whitman, Walt. Song of Myself (1892 Version)," Section 46. *Poetry Foundation*, www.poetryfoundation.org/poems/45477/song-of-myself-1892-version.

[5] "Affective forecasting" is our prediction of how we will feel (affect) in the future. We often base our choices on how we think that choice will affect our emotional state. For more, see Gilbert, Daniel T. *Stumbling on happiness*. Alfred A. Knopf., 2006.

[6] In Jonathan Haidt's words, we are all hypocrites. I see this as all the more reason to be gentle with ourselves and others. For more, see Haidt, Jonathan. *The Happiness Hypothesis: Finding Modern Truth in Ancient Wisdom*. Basic Books, 2005.

[7] Among other wonderful works by Vaillant, see Vaillant, George E, *Aging Well*, Boston, Little Brown, 2002.

[8] For more in general, see Keltner, Dacher. *Born to Be Good: The Science of a Meaningful Life*. New York: W.W. Norton & Co, 2009.

The Great White

Previous versions of this essay appeared on Psychology Today: https://www.psychologytoday.com/us/blog/luminous-things/201706/sharks-and-stoics and at the author's website: http://www.johnseandoyle.com/sharks-and-stoics/

[9] A key premise of cognitive behavioral therapy is that our thoughts about the things and events of our lives, lead to an emotional reaction or other behavioral consequences. To enhance wellbeing and increase resilience and effectiveness, people are taught to separate the "Activating Event" (in this essay, the shark) from their "Beliefs" about that event. (e.g., the shark is a threat). If they can distinguish between the two, they can change their belief and thus, affect a different "Consequence" (emotional response, behavior, etc.). This is referred to as the ABC Model.

Bad Breath

[10] George Vaillant, M.D., points out that "In metaphor (and probably in neuroanatomic fact), the cingulate gyrus [part of the limbic system] links valence and memory to create attachment and along with the hippocampus is the brain region most responsible for making the past meaningful. The anterior cingulate is crucial in directing whom we should approach and whom we should avoid. Maternal touch, body warmth, and odor via the limbic system, and especially via the anterior cingulate, regulate a rat pup's behavior, nerochecmistry, endocrine release and circdain rhythm." (Spiritual Evolution, p. 34) Further, "Love lives within the limbic medial temporal lobe - where smells, music, caretaking and memory all come together - and most especially in the limbic system's anterior cingulate gyrus (Panksepp, 1998). The unifying affect of joy, of awe, of the transcendent appears to arise from limbic structures (Panksepp, 1998)." Positive Emotions, Spirituality and the Practice of Psychiatry, George E. Vaillant, M.D., Mens Sana Monogr. 2008 Jan-Dec; 6(1): 48–62 http://www.ncbi.nlm.nih.gov/pmc/articles/PMC3190563/

[11] The poet-prophet Walt Whitman sang "The scent of these armpits, an aroma finer than prayer." Whitman, Walt. "Song of Myself (1892 Version)," Section 24. *Poetry Foundation*, www.poetryfoundation.org/poems/45477/song-of-myself-1892-version.

[12] We all have certain biases that both help and hinder us as we navigate the world. Our "confirmation bias" is where we tend to notice, remember or highlight the

evidence that supports our preexisting beliefs or hypotheses. It also causes us to discount any information that detracts from what we believe.

[13] According to Carol Dweck, a "fixed mindset" is one in which we assume that our character, intelligence, creativity, leadership or other qualities are static and unmalleable. We believe we cannot change them in any meaningful way. Success in the given domain is an affirmation of something fixed and inherent. Challenges or "failures" delineate the limits of our abilities. By contrast, a "growth mindset," sees our various qualities as pliant and plastic. It leads us to seek out challenges and see "failures" not as evidence of limits, but as opportunities to stretch and grow. These types of mindset are domain specific. For example, we might have a growth mindset about intelligence, but a fixed mindset about creativity. In most contexts, a growth mindset contributes significantly to our personal and professional success, the health of our relationships and ultimately our capacity for happiness. Dweck, Carol S. *Mindset: the new psychology of success*. Ballantine Books, 2008.

[14] Physicist Pierre Duhem, and philosopher Willard Van Orman Quine both noticed that scientists will explain the same scientific data and other evidence with different theories. According to the Duhem–Quine thesis, even in scientific inquiries, "theories are underdetermined by the evidence." For more on the Duhem–Quine thesis, see: Stanford, Kyle, "*Underdetermination of Scientific Theory*", The Stanford Encyclopedia of Philosophy (Winter 2017 Edition), Edward N. Zalta (ed.), https://plato.stanford.edu/archives/win2017/entries/scientific-underdetermination/.

[15] Ellen Langer points out that our initial exposure to information can lead to "mindless" processing of that information and its subsequent use. Because such mindsets form before we do much reflection, we call them premature cognitive commitments. Examples include many believes about old age. Long before we consider ourselves old, we are given negative stereotypes about aging. At the time the information seems personally irrelevant, and we tuck it away unconsciously without ever testing its limits, or questioning whether it is true at all. Subjects primed with stereotypes about aging – forgetfulness, Florida, bingo – then walk more slowly when leaving the testing center. However, people exposed to more optimistic images of aging, are likely to have a richer experience in old age. Langer, Ellen. *Mindfulness*. Da Capo Press, 1990.

[16] We can't always trust our feelings, or even our unconscious biological responses to the world. In classic example of "misattribution of arousal", researchers approached male subjects either on a high, cable suspension bridge or on a low, sturdy one. In each condition, the men crossing the bridge were met by a female experimenter who asked them to tell stories about a set of pictures. She also gave the men her phone number "just in case you have any questions". The men who met the experimenter on the suspension bridge told stories with greater sexual content and were more likely to call their inquisitress. At some level, the subjects believed that the sense of arousal they felt from being suspended, swinging above a gorge, was due to the female experimenter. Fear is not the only emotion that can be a result of misattribution of arousal. Dutton,

Donald. G. and Aron, Arnold. P. "Some evidence for heightened sexual attraction under conditions of high anxiety". *Journal of Personality and Social Psychology*. 30 (4): 1974, pp. 510–517. Daniel Kahneman gives an example about the value doubting the things that seem intuitively obvious. In studies, people are told a baseball bat and ball cost a total of $1.10, and that the bat costs $1 more than the ball. When asked how much the ball cost, most people rely on their intuition and incorrectly say $0.10. However, this is incorrect. (If the ball were $0.10 and the bat were $1.0 more, the total would be $1.20. The ball in Kahneman's example costs $0.05). Just as with the bat and ball example, when I experienced things in school as difficult, my intuition gave me one answer that I never released I could question. See Kahneman, Daniel. *Thinking, fast and slow*. Farrar, Straus and Giroux, 2015.

[17] Martin Seligman gives another example how we are often biased toward negative appraisals of certain facts about our worlds. Doris Kearns Goodwin, the biographer of Eleanor Roosevelt, said that the first lady devoted a great potion of her life to helping people of color *"to compensate for her mother's narcissism and her father's alcoholism."* Goodwin, says Seligman, never considered the possibility that Eleanor Roosevelt was, deep down, acting out of goodness. Seligman goes on further to state that *"there is a not a shred of evidence that strength and virtue are derived from negative motivation."* Seligman, Martin E. P. *Authentic happiness: using the new positive psychology to realize your potential for lasting fulfillment*. New York: Free Press, 2002.

[18] John O'Donohue one said it is *"my suspicion is that the soul choreographs one's biography and one's destiny . . . it often seems to me here that a person believes that if they tell you their story, that's who they are. And sometimes these stories are constructed with the most banal second-hand psychological and spiritual cliché, and you look at a beautiful interesting face telling a story that you know doesn't hold a candle to the life that's secretly in there. So what I think happens here a bit is that there's a reduction of identity to biography. And they're not the same thing. I think biography unfolds identity and makes it visible and puts the mirror of it out there, but I think identity is a more complex thing."* O'Donohue, John, "The Inner Landscape of Beauty." *On Being*, https://onbeing.org/programs/john-odonohue-the-inner-landscape-of-beauty/.

[19] In an extensively researched paper, Roy Baumeister and his colleagues point out that *"The greater power of bad events over good ones is found in everyday events, major life events (e.g., trauma), close relationship outcomes, social network patterns, interpersonal interactions, and learning processes. Bad emotions, bad parents, and bad feedback have more impact than good ones, and bad information is processed more thoroughly than good. The self is more motivated to avoid bad self-definitions than to pursue good ones. Bad impressions and bad stereotypes are quicker to form and more resistant to disconfirmation than good ones. Various explanations such as diagnosticity and salience help explain some findings, but the greater power of bad events is still found when such variables are controlled. Hardly any exceptions (indicating greater power of good) can be found. Taken together, these findings suggest that bad is*

stronger than good, as a general principle across a broad range of psychological phenomena." Baumeister, Roy, et al. "Bad is Stronger Than Good." *Review of General Psychology*, vol. 5, no. 4, 2001, pp. 323–370. http://assets.csom.umn.edu/assets/71516.pdf

[20] "*Couples who are happy in their relationship have a 5:1 ratio of positive to negative during conflict conversations and a 20:1 positive to negative ratio when just hanging out. Relationships have to be a very rich climate of positivity to feel good: lots of kindness, attention, interest in one another, affection, humor, good sex and so on.*" - Drs. John and Julie Gottman
https://www.facebook.com/GottmanInstitute/posts/10150569358225865

[21] Attributed to Goethe. See Frankl, Viktor. "Why believe in others." *TED: Ideas worth spreading,* www.ted.com/talks/viktor_frankl_youth_in_search_of_meaning/discussion.

[22] For more beautiful and wonderful stories about how the little things people do, can have big, dramatic effects, see https://daymakermovement.com/

Part II. Being Toward Others

Refuge in Love

Versions of this essay previously appeared on Positive Psychology News Daily: http://positivepsychologynews.com/news/sean-doyle/2013032525681, on the author's website here: http://www.johnseandoyle.com/an-argument-for-kindness-part-i/ and here: http://www.johnseandoyle.com/an-argument-for-kindness-part-ii/ and in the author's *Being Human: A chapbook of selected essays. A love letter.* lulu.com (September 18, 2015)

[23] See Cacioppo, John T., et al. "Alone in the Crowd: The Structure and Spread of Loneliness in a Large Social Network." *Journal of Personality and Social Psychology,* 2009, pp. 977–991. See also Christakis, Nicholas A. & Fowler, James H., *Connected: The Surprising Power of Our Social Networks and How They Shape Our Lives.* New York: Little, Brown, 2009.

[24] This essay was heavily influenced by Nagler, Michael, *Is There No Other Way? The Search for a Nonviolent Future.* Berkley Hill Books: Berkley, 2001.

[25] Vaillant, George E. *Spiritual Evolution: A Scientific Defense of Faith.* New York: Broadway Press, 2008.

[26] For more, also see generally, Heschel, Abraham Joshua. *God in Search of Man: a Philosophy of Judaism.* Farrar, Straus and Giroux, 1999.

What Ever Happened to Conner MacBride

A version of this essay first appeared on the author's website, at http://www.johnseandoyle.com/conner-macbride/ and in the author's *Being Human: A chapbook of selected essays. A love letter.* lulu.com (September 18, 2015)

Absence and Return

A version of this essay first appeared on the author's website, at http://www.johnseandoyle.com/absence-and-return/.

[27] There is often a disconnect between what we believe, what we feel and how we act. Most of the time, it *feels* like our lives are special, and in some way, more important that the lives of others. In *Le Père Goriot* by Honoré de Balzac, the hero asks "What would you do if you had the possibility to become instantaneously rich, under the sole condition that, by simply willing, without anybody knowing, you would kill a mandarin in China?" In *Cosmopolitanism: Ethics in a World of Strangers* (W. W. Norton & Company, Mar 1, 2010) moral philosopher Kwame Anthony Appiah points out that troubling question appears to be inspired by a dilemma proposed by Adam Smith in *The Theory of Moral Sentiments*. "Let us suppose that the great empire of China, with all its myriads of inhabitants, was suddenly swallowed up by an earthquake, and let us consider how a man of humanity in Europe, who had no sort of connexion [sic] with that part of the world, would be affected upon receiving intelligence of this dreadful calamity. He would, I imagine, first of all, express very strongly his sorrow for the misfortune of that unhappy people, he would make many melancholy reflections upon the precariousness of human life, and the vanity of all the labours of man, which could thus be annihilated in a moment. He would too, perhaps, if he was a man of speculation, enter into many reasonings concerning the effects which this disaster might produce upon the commerce of Europe, and the trade and business of the world in general. And when all this fine philosophy was over, when all these humane sentiments had been once fairly expressed, he would pursue his business or his pleasure, take his repose or his diversion, with the same ease and tranquility [sic], as if no such accident had happened. The most frivolous disaster which could befal [sic] himself would occasion a more real disturbance. If he was to lose his little finger to-morrow, he would not sleep to-night; but, provided he never saw them, he will snore with the most profound security over the ruin of a hundred millions of his brethren, and the destruction of that immense multitude seems plainly an object less interesting to him, than this paltry misfortune of his own. To prevent, therefore, this paltry misfortune to himself, would a man of humanity be willing to sacrifice the lives of a hundred millions of his brethren, provided he had never seen them? Human nature startles with horror at the thought, and the world, in its greatest depravity and corruption, never produced such a villain as could be capable of entertaining it. " Quote from: http://www.econlib.org/library/Smith/smMS3.html

Sacred Thread

A version of this essay first appeared on the author's website, at http://www.johnseandoyle.com/the-sacred-thread/

[28] Prabhavananda. *The Upanishads: Breath of the Eternal: the Principal Texts*. Translated by Frederick Manchester, New American Library, 2002.

[29] Kazantzakis, Nikos. *The Saviors of God; Spiritual Exercises*. Simon and Schuster, 1960.

Throwing Bullets in the Fire

Versions of this essay previously appeared on Psychology Today at https://www.psychologytoday.com/us/blog/luminous-things/201505/throwing-bullets-the-fire and on the author's website at http://www.johnseandoyle.com/throwing-bullets/.

Part III. Overcoming and Acceptance

Lost at Sea

A version of this essay first appeared on the author's website, at http://www.johnseandoyle.com/survival-at-sea-in-business-and-in-life/

[30] See Tough, Paul. "A Speck in the Sea." *The New York Times Magazine*, 5 Jan. 2014, mobile.nytimes.com/2014/01/05/magazine/a-speck-in-the-sea.html.

[31] http://www.paultough.com/

[32] See, Sherwood, Ben. *The Survivors Club: The Secrets and Science that Could Save Your Life*. Grand Central Publishing, 2009 . pp 128-29.

[33] Synder, Charles R., et. al. "Hope Theory: A Member of the Positive Psychology Family." In Lopez, Shane J., and Charles R. Snyder. *Handbook of positive psychology*. Oxford Univ. Press, 2002.

[34] Maddox, J. E., "Self-Efficacy: The power in believing you can." In Lopez, Shane J., and Charles R. Snyder. Handbook of positive psychology. Oxford Univ. Press, 2002.

[35] For Snyder, hope is not just a feeling or an emotion, but it is a thinking process. We have (1) goals that provide a direction and endpoint toward which we are moving, (2) pathways are the routes we identify and create to achieve our desired goals (3) agency refers to our perceived efficacy and capacity to use those pathways to reach desired goals. When faced with the inevitable (4) barriers to the attainment of our goals, we can either give up or we can use our pathway and agency thoughts to create new

routes. Synder, Charles R., et. al. "Hope Theory: A Member of the Positive Psychology Family." In Lopez, Shane J., and Charles R. Snyder. *Handbook of positive psychology.* Oxford Univ. Press, 2002.

It Is Not the Mountain We Conquer

[36] The title of this essay is from a quote by George Mallory: "*It is not the mountain we conquer, but ourselves.*"

[37] From, *Musee des Beaux Arts,* by W.H Auden.

[38] The Barron-Hulleman Expectancy-Value-Costs model of motivation recognizes the important role of three components in promoting overall motivation: (i) having an *expectancy* of being successful in a task, (ii) having sufficient *value* for engaging in the task, and (iii) a relatively low *cost* of engaging in an activity. Barron, Kenneth E. & Hulleman, Christopher S., "Expectancy-Value-Cost Model of Motivation." In: James D. Wright (editor-in-chief), *International Encyclopedia of the Social & Behavioral Sciences,* 2nd edition, Vol 8. Oxford: Elsevier. 2015, pp. 503–509

[39] On whether he thought they could climb Mt. Everest, Edmund Hillary said: "*Never, at any stage, until we actually got up the rock step, was I confident that we were going to be successful. My feeling was that we would give it everything we had, but we had no surety that we were going to reach the top. In fact, I believe that if someone starts out on a challenging activity, completely confident that they're going to succeed, why bother starting? It's not much of a challenge. I think it's much better to start out on something that you're not at all sure that you can do. If you overcome and you manage to defeat the obstacles, the satisfaction is so much greater.*"

[40] When asked why he would attempt to climb Mt. Everest, George Mallory said "*So, if you cannot understand that there is something in man which responds to the challenge of this mountain and goes out to meet it, that the struggle is the struggle of life itself upward and forever upward, then you won't see why we go. What we get from this adventure is just sheer joy. And joy is, after all, the end of life. We do not live to eat and make money. We eat and make money to be able to enjoy life. That is what life means and what life is for.*" From, Mallory, George Leigh. *Climbing Everest: the Complete Writings of George Mallory.* Gibson Square Books Ltd, 2012.

To Repair with Gold

Versions of this essay previously appeared at https://www.psychologytoday.com/us/blog/luminous-things/201510/resilience-growth-kintsukuroi and http://www.johnseandoyle.com/kintsukuroi/ and in the author's *Being Human: A chapbook of selected essays. A love letter.* lulu.com (September 18, 2015).

[41] See generally, Culin, Katherine R. Von, et al. "Unpacking Grit: Motivational Correlates of Perseverance and Passion for Long-Term Goals." *The Journal of Positive Psychology*, vol. 9, no. 4, 2014, pp. 306–312 and Duckworth, Angela, *Grit: The Power of Passion and Perseverance*. Scribner, 2013.

[42] *Sisu* is a Finnish concept comprised of various constructs including stoic determination, tenacity of purpose, grit, bravery, resilience and hardiness. Lahti, Emilia. *Above and Beyond Perseverance: An Exploration of Sisu* (Master's thesis). University of Pennsylvania. 2013.

[43] While most people are familiar with posttraumatic stress syndrome, and coping, researchers have found that some people, experience great positive in the face of trauma. Tedeschi and Calhoun point out that "posttraumatic growth" typically occurs in any of five areas: (1) a sense that new opportunities have emerged from the struggle that were not present before, (2) an experience stronger closer relationships with others and an increased sense of connection to others who suffer, (3) an increased sense of one's own strength – "if I lived through that, what can life throw at me that I cannot handle?", (4) a greater appreciation for life in general, or (5) a deepening of one's spiritual lives, including a significant change in one's belief system. For more, see Post Traumatic Growth, Tedeschi, Richard G., et. al. *Post-traumatic growth Some needed corrections and reminders*. European Journal of Personality, 28, 2014 , pp. 350-351, and Tedeschi, Richard G., & Calhoun, Lawrence G. *Posttraumatic growth: Conceptual foundations and empirical evidence*. Psychological Inquiry, 15(1), 2004, pp. 1-18.

[44] Kaufman, Scott Barry. "Are You Mentally Tough?" *Scientific American Blog Network*, 19 Mar. 2014, Retrieved 14:35, October 3, 2015 from http://blogs.scientificamerican.com/beautiful-minds/are-you-mentally-tough/.

[45] For more, see Kintsugi. *In Wikipedia, The Free Encyclopedia*. Sept. 28, 2015. Retrieved 14:28, October 3, 2015, from https://en.wikipedia.org/w/index.php?title=Kintsugi&oldid=683186968

[46] Kushner, Harold. *When bad things happen to good people*. New York: Schocken Books, 1981.

[47] See http://anomalyinfo.com/Stories/gratitude-crane-japanese-legend.

[48] "In the Tang Dynasty, the weaving goddess floated down on a shaft of moonlight with her two attendants, showed to the upright court official Guo Han in his garden that a goddess's robe is seamless for it is woven without the use of needle and thread, entirely on the loom. The phrase 'a goddess's robe is seamless' passed into an idiom to express perfect workmanship." See http://www.crystalinks.com/weaving_goddess.html.

[49] In Baltic mythology, Saule, the life-affirming sun goddess, spins the sunbeams on a wheel or rosette. See http://www.crystalinks.com/weaving_goddess.html.

[50] See Homer, *The Odyssey.*

[51] The VIA Institute on Character, graciously granted me permission to use their summaries of various psychological studies found on their site: https://www.viacharacter.org/www.

[52] Emmons, R. A., & McCullough, M. E. (2003). Counting blessings versus burdens: An experimental investigation of gratitude and subjective well-being in daily life. Journal of Personality and Social Psychology, 84, 377–389.

[53] Id.

[54] McCullough, M. E., Emmons, R. A., & Tsang, J. (2002). The grateful disposition: A conceptual and empirical topography. Journal of Personality and Social Psychology, 82, 112-127. See https://www.viacharacter.org/.

[55] The character strengths most associated with the meaning route to happiness are religiousness, gratitude, hope, zest, and curiosity (Peterson et al., 2007). Peterson, C., Ruch, W., Beerman, U., Park, N., & Seligman, M. E. P. (2007). Strengths of character, orientations to happiness, and life satisfaction. Journal of Positive Psychology, 2, 149-156. See https://www.viacharacter.org/

[56] The five strengths are hope (r = .53), zest (r = .52), gratitude (r = .43), curiosity (r = .39), and love (r = .35). These strengths consistently and repeatedly show a robust, consistent relationship with life satisfaction. The correlations given were from a sample of 3907 individuals; see article for data on two additional samples. Park, N., Peterson, C., & Seligman, M. E. P. (2004). Strengths of character and well-being. Journal of Social & Clinical Psychology, 23, 603–619. The benefits of gratitude don't end there. In school, high levels of gratitude predicts high GPAs. See Park, N., & Peterson, C. (2008a). Positive psychology and character strengths: Application to strengths-based school counseling. Professional School Counseling, 12 (2), 85-92. Along with perseverance, fairness, honesty, hope, and perspective, after controlling for IQ. See also, Park, N., & Peterson, C. (2009a). Character strengths: Research and practice. Journal of College and Character, 10 (4), np. The character strengths – perseverance, love, gratitude, and hope – predict academic achievement in middle school students and college students. At work, gratitude leads to greater job satisfaction. See Peterson, C., Stephens, J. P., Park, N., Lee, F., & Seligman, M. E. P. (2010). Strengths of character and work. Oxford handbook of positive psychology and work. In Linley, P. A., Harrington, S., & Garcea, N. (Eds.). Oxford handbook of positive psychology and work (pp. 221-231). New York: Oxford University Press. Along with curiosity, zest, hope, and spirituality, across occupations. See also, Gorjian, N. (2006). Virtue of transcendence in relation to work orientation, job satisfaction and turnover cognitions. Dissertation Abstracts International: Section B:

The Sciences and Engineering, 67 (2-B), 1190. Among 226 employees, the strengths under the virtue of transcendence – hope, humor, gratitude, and spirituality (not appreciation of beauty/excellence) – had a direct positive relationship with a calling work orientation. Further, People who are grateful have more good feelings and vitality and less depression and envy. See McCullough, M. E., Emmons, R. A., & Tsang, J. (2002). The grateful disposition: A conceptual and empirical topography. Journal of Personality and Social Psychology, 82, 112-127. See https://www.viacharacter.org/

[57] We can have a deep sense of gratitude, regardless of our beliefs about god. There are some faith traditions that hold that if we believe in a God, then we can never reject any of the facts of life: The losses; the pains; every act of unkindness. The buddhas, prophets and avatars all knew, that the whole of the universe, and everything in it, is divine. Everything is a manifestation of divinity. If we do not have a belief in God, we can still feel deeply grateful. When this life and everything in it is all we have, how can we let the simple fact of suffering or brutality, vulgarity or thoughtlessness, also take away our joy? Albert Camus is purported to have said there is a "moral imperative" to being happy, when we have nothing but this moment.

[58] The "Eternity" against which we find ourselves isn't some later time or long infinite chain running forward into forever. *"Eternity has nothing to do with time. Eternity is that dimension of here and now which thinking in time cuts out . . . this is it . . . If you don't get it here, you won't get it anywhere, and the experience of eternity right here and now is the function of life.* Campbell, Joseph. "Ep. 2: Joseph Campbell and the Power of Myth -- 'The Message of the Myth'." *BillMoyers.com*, 22 June 1988, billmoyers.com/content/ep-2-joseph-campbell-and-the-power-of-myth-the-message-of-the-myth. The idea is to realize both your identity with eternity and your participation in the present time. Rather than withdraw from the world when you realize how horrible it can be, recognize that the horror is simply part of it all, and that there is a great wonder in just participating in the whole, infinite drama.

[59] *Last night as, I was sleeping / I dreamt-marvellous [sic] error!- / that I had a beehive / here inside my heart. / And the golden bees / were making white combs / and sweet honey / from all my old failures.* Machado, Antonio. *Times Alone: Selected Poems of Antonio Machado.* Translated by Robert Bly, Wesleyan University Press, 1983. p. 43

[60] *Who is it who throws light into the meeting on the mountain? / Who announces the ages of the moon? / Who teaches the place where couches the sun? (If not I?).* Montague, John, ed., "Song of Amergin." *Book of Irish Verse: An Anthology of Irish Poetry from the 6th Century to the Present.*, Peter Smith Pub Inc, 1984.

[61] See *Legends of the Quran: Solomon's Flying Carpet*, www.answering-islam.org/Quran/Sources/Legends/flying_carpet.htm.

[62] In work that they published in 2004, Anthony Ong and Cindy Bergeman explored the emotional experiences of 40 adults from 60 to 85 years old. They asked them to

keep diaries of their emotional experiences for 30 days, identifying experienced emotions and their intensities. They found that the people who are most vulnerable to stress tended to be unidimensional in their experience of emotions, that is, they experienced emotions on a single continuum from good to bad. They also looked at individuals who test high for resilience, and found that they can have positive emotions and negative emotions at the same time, even while experiencing personally significant stress. They were also better able to differentiate their emotions. When people can feel positive emotions at the same time that they feel negative emotions, they are less vulnerable to the effects of stress. Ong, A. N. (2010). Pathways Linking Positive Emotion and Health in Later Life. Current Directions in Psychological Science, 19(6), 358-362. Ong, A. N., Bergeman, C. S., Bisconti, T. L. & Wallace, K. A. (2006). Psychological resilience, positive emotions, and successful adaptation to stress in later life. Journal of Personality and Social Psychology, 91 (4), 730–749 Ong, A. N. & Bergeman, C. S. (2004). The Complexity of Emotions in Later Life. Journal of Gerontology, 59B (3), 117–122. See https://www.viacharacter.org/

[63] The poet W.B. Yeats said that it requires a "mature intellect" to "hold in a single thought reality and justice." For F. Scott Fitzgerald, the *test of a first-rate intelligence is the ability to hold two opposed ideas in mind at the same time and still retain the ability to function. One should, for example, be able to see that things are hopeless and yet be determined to make them otherwise."* Neuroendocrinologist Robert Sapolsky, says that what makes us the most human is our ability to hold contradictory things in our head at the same time, and make them vital and imperative precisely because they are contradictory. Sapolsky, Robert. "The uniqueness of humans." | TED Talk, www.ted.com/talks/robert_sapolsky_the_uniqueness_of_humans.

[64] Thank you to Jundo Cohen of Treeleaf Zendo, who first introduced me to John Daido Loori Roshi and his ideas concerning "great gratitude".

[65] Heschel, Abraham Joshua. *God in Search of Man: a Philosophy of Judaism.* Farrar, Straus and Giroux, 1999. p. 49.

Part IV. Embracing It All

Earthworms and Puddles

A version of this essay previously appeared on Positive Psychology News Daily, found here: http://positivepsychologynews.com/news/sean-doyle/2013042325827

[66] Sapolsky, Robert. *Why Zebras Don't Get Ulcers,* Holt Paperbacks; 3rd edition (August 26, 2004).

[67] Zagajewski, Adam. Tierra del fuego. In *Mysticism for Beginners.* Farrar, Straus and Giroux. 1997.

[68] See http://www.potteryali.com/

[69] All the onion quotes in this passage from, Neruda, Pablo. "Ode to an Onion". In *Fifty Odes*, Host Publications, 2006.

Secret Destinations

[70] The ways in which we develop our earliest attachments shapes our perceptions and expectations about the self and future relationships. Over time, we build on these internal working models, and they shape the extent to which we feel we are worthy of being loved and believe others will be there for us when needed. For more on attachment theory, see: Ainsworth, Mary D. Salter, et. al. *Patterns of attachment: A psychological study of the strange situation*. Hillsdale, NJ: Lawrence Erlbaum Associates, Inc., 1978. Interestingly, new research suggests that people can change their attachment style over time and feel better about their relationships. Stanton, Sarah C. E., et al. "Benefits of Positive Relationship Experiences for Avoidantly Attached Individuals." *Journal of Personality and Social Psychology*, vol. 113, no. 4, 2017, pp. 568–588.

[71] Self-determination theory posits that there are three psychological needs we all must meet (autonomy, competence, and relatedness) to maintain optimal performance and well-being. For more see Deci, Edward L., and Ryan, Richard M. *Intrinsic motivation and self-determination in human behavior*. Plenum, New York, NY, 1985; and Deci, Edward L., and Ryan, Richard M. "Self-determination theory and the facilitation of intrinsic motivation, social development, and well-being." *American Psychologist*, 55, 2000, pp. 68-78.

[72] The need to form and maintain strong, stable relationships, and have frequent, positive interactions within them, has a powerful effect on our well-being. See Baumeister, Roy F., and Mark R. Leary. "The Need to Belong: Desire for Interpersonal Attachments as a Fundamental Human Motivation." *Psychological Bulletin*, vol. 117, no. 3, 1995, pp. 497–529.

[73] Probably the most well-known theory of needs, is from Maslow. See Maslow, Abraham H. *A theory of human motivation*. Psychological review,50(4), 1943, pp. 370. See also Maslow, Abraham. H. *Toward a psychology of being*. Start Publishing LLC. 2013.

[74] It does not feel good, but I believe as strongly as I do about anything in life, that one of the greatest things we can do for our own development, well-being, and psychological and spiritual growth, is to seek out things that push us or make us uncomfortable, **and to find a way to rejoice as we are struggling through them.** Socrates was said to endure the insults and nagging of his wife Xanthippe "*Because, when I put up with her at home, such as she is, I develop a tolerance from the exercise, which allows me to bear a bit more lightly the insults and injustices of the outside world.*" Aulus Gellius, *Attic Nights* 1.17. And of course, Kierkegaard looked out at

the world and said: *"So there I sat and smoked my cigar until I drifted into thought. Among other thoughts, I recall these. You are getting on in years, I said to myself, and are becoming an old man without being anything and without actually undertaking anything. On the other hand, wherever you look in literature or in life, you see the names and figures of celebrities, the prized and highly acclaimed people, prominent or much discussed, the many benefactors of the age who know how to benefit humankind by making life easier and easier, some by railroads, others by omnibuses and steamships, others by telegraph, others by easily understood surveys and brief publications about everything worth knowing, and finally the true benefactors of the age who by virtue of thought systematically make spiritual existence easier and easier and yet more and more meaningful—and what are you doing? . . . So only one lack remains [in our time], even though not yet felt, the lack of difficulty. Out of love of humankind, out of despair over my awkward predicament of having achieved nothing and of being unable to make anything easier than it had already been made, out of genuine interest in those who make everything easy,* **I comprehended that it was my task: to make difficulties everywhere.**" (emphasis added) – Søren Kierkegaard, *Concluding Unscientific Postscript to Philosophical Fragments,* 1846.

[75] In the Stanford Prison Experiment, psychologist Philip Zimbardo randomly assigned student volunteers to act as either prison guards or inmates. Despite each subject having passed diagnostic interviews and psychological tests, the experiment had to be terminated early because the "guards" were abusing the "prisoners". See http://www.prisonexp.org/, Haney, Craig, et al., "Interpersonal dynamics in a simulated prison." *International Journal of Criminology and Penology,* 1973.

[76] When in March 2004, it was discovered that US soldiers had been abusing detainees in the Abu Ghraib prison in Iraq, psychologist Phillip Zimbardo noted the similarities between it and the Stanford Prison Experiment. In each situation, otherwise psychologically healthy people did not know how to act in unfamiliar circumstances and were vulnerable to influence. See, Zimbardo, Phillip, *The Lucifer Effect: Understanding How Good People Turn Evil,* Random House, 2007.

[77] Research on bystander intervention has produced a great number of studies showing that the presence of other people in a critical situation reduces the likelihood that an individual will help. See, Fischer, Peter, et. al., "The bystander-effect: A meta-analytic review on bystander intervention in dangerous and non-dangerous emergencies". *Psychological Bulletin.* 137 (4): 517–537.
 http://psycnet.apa.org/doiLanding?doi=10.1037%2Fa0023304

[78] After the Nuremburg Trials of Nazi war criminals, psychologist Stanley Milgram conducted an experiment to examine how such atrocities could have occurred. Subjects were told to administer electric shocks of increasing intensity to another person outside of their view. The dial was marked with safety warnings at the higher voltages and the people purportedly receiving the punishment would scream as the shocks were administered. While no one actually received the shocks, every participant complied with instructions to turn the dial to dangerous levels. Roughly

two-thirds continued to the highest, fatal level of 450 volts. Milgram, Stanley. "Behavioral Study of obedience." *The Journal of Abnormal and Social Psychology*, 67(4), 1963, pp. 371-378. http://dx.doi.org/10.1037/h0040525

[79] After analyzing all the airplane accidents between 1983 and 2000, The National Transportation Safety Board reported that there was a survival rate of 95.7. In its own study the European Transport Safety Council reported that 40 percent of the fatalities that did occur in plane crashes were survivable. Because of their unfamiliarity with the circumstances, an alarming number of people failed to act and remained buckled in their seats. Sherwood, Ben. "Chapter 3: Ninety Seconds to Save Your Life: The Wrong (and Right) Things To Do In A Plane Crash." *The Survivors Club: The Secrets and Science that Could Save Your Life*. Grand Central Publishing, 2009.

[80] See Boorstin, Daniel J., "Chapter 3: From Traveler to Tourist, the Lost Art of Travel." *The Image: A guide to pseudo-events in America*. Atheneum, 1987, p. 103.

[81] Id., p 84. Remember also Ishmael's shock in *Moby Dick*, when he discovered he was sharing a bed with Queequeg, a "abominable savage" and "peddler of heads."

Adventures Just Outside Your Door

Versions of this essay previously appeared on Psychology Today here: https://www.psychologytoday.com/us/blog/luminous-things/201703/rediscovering-zest-life and on the author's website, here:
http://www.johnseandoyle.com/rediscovering-a-zest-for-life/

[82] This quote, and more on "microadventures", can be found at Humphreys, Alastair . "Microadventures." www.alastairhumphreys.com/microadventures-3/.

[83] See *Secret Destinations*, above.

[84] The character strengths most highly related to life satisfaction are hope (r = .53), zest (r = .52), gratitude (r = .43), curiosity (r = .39), and love (r = .35). These strengths consistently and repeatedly show a robust, consistent relationship with life satisfaction. Park, N., Peterson, C., & Seligman, M. E. P. (2004). Strengths of character and well-being. *Journal of Social & Clinical Psychology*, 23, 603–619. See https://www.viacharacter.org/

[85] When compared with U.S. adults, youth from the U.S. are higher on the character strengths of hope, teamwork, and zest and adults are higher on appreciation of beauty & excellence, honesty, leadership, open-mindedness. Park, N., & Peterson, C. (2006). Moral competence and character strengths among adolescents: The development and validation of the Values in Action Inventory of Strengths for Youth. *Journal of Adolescence*, 29, 891-905. See https://www.viacharacter.org/

[86] See *Horizons*, above.

[87] See *Secret Destinations*, above.

Endgame

A version of this essay previously appeared on the author's website at http://www.johnseandoyle.com/endgame/.

[88] Bergman, Ingmar, director. *The seventh seal.* Svensk Filmindustri, 1956.

[89] The artist Marcel Duchamp was so obsessed with chess that "[o]n his honeymoon, he analyzed chess problems until, it is said, one night, in a rage, his wife glued the pieces to the board." Edmonds, David, and John Eidinow. *Bobby Fischer goes to war: how the Soviets lost the most extraordinary chess match of all time.* Ecco, 2005.

[90] "I feel as if I were a piece in a game of chess, when my opponent says of it: That piece cannot be moved." Kierkegaard, Søren. *Either/Or.* Princeton University Press, 1987.

[91] Philosopher and writer Jean-Paul Sartre even asserted that "*Never were we freer than under the German occupation. We had lost all our rights, and first of all our right to speak. They insulted us to our faces. ... They deported us en masse. ... And because of all this we were free... [Fore] the choice that each one made of his life was authentic.*" Sartre, Jean-Paul. "*Paris Alive: The Republic of Silence.*" The Atlantic Monthly, Dec. 1944, p. 43.

[92] For further reading, see Edmonds, David, and John Eidinow. *Bobby Fischer goes to war: how the Soviets lost the most extraordinary chess match of all time.* Ecco, 2005.

The Beautiful Game

For the author's TEDx talk on the Beautiful Game, please see https://www.youtube.com/watch?v=0GWLEH8-1rM&t=13s.

[93] Playing off this, one of the major shoe companies adopted the phrase Joga Bonito or "play it beautifully" or "he plays it beautifully" and used many of the Brazilian and other stars in its adds

[94] Coach Carlos Alberto Parreira was criticized for abandoning Brazil's engaging style, known as the beautiful game, and for relying on a more cautious, defensive posture reflecting modern soccer. It seemed not to matter that Parreira had brought Brazil a World Cup title in 1994. *O Globo,* a leading Rio daily, described Parreira's current style as "football without fun, without life, without joy, without personality, without the Brazilian way of playing." The newspaper *Folha de São Paulo* called *Parreira* a "complete disaster." One of its columnists wrote that "anyone who refuses to play the beautiful game deserves every punishment."

http://www.nytimes.com/2006/07/03/sports/soccer/03brazil.html   See   also
http://www.nytimes.com/2014/07/08/sports/worldcup/world-cup-2014-brazil-
eschews-the-beautiful-game-for-more-rugged-style.html?_r=0

[95] Whitman, Walt. Song of Myself (1892 Version)", Section 24. *Poetry Foundation*,
www.poetryfoundation.org/poems/45477/song-of-myself-1892-version.

[96] Camus argues that if we have only this lifetime, then we have a moral obligation to
be happy. Heschel urges us to "Remember that there is meaning beyond absurdity.
Know that every deed counts, that every word is power...Above all, remember that
you must build your life as if it were a work of art."

[97] "Play introduces us to the social, emotional and physical skills needed to make the
most of our life. Indeed, play is regarded as a 'form of practice, or proximal growth, or
mastery of skills' Lutz, S., "Mapping the wellspring of a positive life: The importance
of measure to the movement". *Gallup Review*, 3, 2000, p. 33, cited in Lopez, Shane J.
Positive Psychology: the Scientific and Practical Explorations of Human Strengths.
3rd ed., Sage Publications, 2015, p. 81. In addition, see Huizinga, Johan. *Homo
Ludens*, 1938, translated as "Playing Man", in which the author discusses the
importance of the play element of culture and society. Finally, see Alan Watts on *the
Fool, the Joker and Monk*: https://www.youtube.com/watch?v=xtHPUThgdyI

God and Intimacy

[98] Exodus, 3:6 "*He said also, "I am the God of your father, the God of Abraham, the
God of Isaac, and the God of Jacob." Then Moses hid his face, for he was afraid to
look at God.*"; Acts 3:13 "*The God of Abraham, Isaac and Jacob, the God of our
fathers, has glorified His servant Jesus, the one whom you delivered and disowned in
the presence of Pilate, when he had decided to release Him.*" Mathew 22:32, "*I Am
the God of Abraham, and the God of Isaac, and the God of Jacob '? He is not the God
of the dead but of the living.*" All quotations from the New American Bible, Revised
Edition, Confraternity of Christian Doctrine, Inc., Washington, D.C., 2010.

[99] See, for example, Haidt, Jonathan *The happiness hypothesis: Finding modern truth
in ancient wisdom*. New York: Basic Books, 2006.

[100] For Job, knowledge without truthfulness is tasteless as the white of an egg. Job 6:6
"*Can something tasteless be eaten without salt, Or is there any taste in the white of an
egg?*" New American Standard Bible

[101] What if instead we listened when the Prophet told not to "defame or abuse others"
but to become "a refuge for humankind, their lives and their properties." "A true
Muslim is the one who does not defame or abuse others; but the truly righteous
becomes a refuge for humankind, their lives and their properties." -Hadith The
Prophet Muhammad SAW as narrated by AbdAllah bin Amr   Retrieved from
http://www.beliefnet.com/Quotes/Islam/Hadith/T/The-Prophet-Muhammad-SAW-

As-Narrated-By-Abdallah-Bin-Amr/A-True-Muslim-Is-The-One-Who-Does-Not-Defame-Or-Ab.aspx#uDWbVrXiAVcqzOBb.99

[102] Or if we tried to save our brothers from their own aggression, regardless of whether they were the oppressor or the oppressed?

[103] "*Whoever destroys a soul, it is considered as if he destroyed an entire world. And whoever saves a life, it is considered as if he saved an entire world.*" Jerusalem Talmud, Sanhedrin 4:1 (22a) See also, the 32nd verse of the fifth Sura, of the Quran: "*And whoever saves a life, it is as though he had saved the lives of all men.*"

[104] Mathew 18:3-4 "*and said, 'Truly I say to you, unless you are converted and become like children, you will not enter the kingdom of heaven. Whoever then humbles himself as this child, he is the greatest in the kingdom of heaven.'* New American Standard Bible.; "*Great is the human who has not lost his childlike heart.*" ~Mencius; "*He who is in harmony with the Tao is like a newborn child.*" Lao Tzu, Tao Te Ching;

[105] "*Kindness is a mark of faith, and whoever has not kindness has not faith.*" As quoted in Al-Islam by Khwajah Kamal al-Din, 1926, p. 47

[106] The Prophet Mohammad SAW

[107] Numerous cultures throughout history told stories of gods changing form and walking among us. "How different was the image of the Other in the epoch of anthropomorphic beliefs, the belief that the gods could assume human form and act like people. Back then you could never tell whether the approaching wanderer, traveler or newcomer was a person or a god in human guise. That uncertainty, that fascinating ambivalence, was one of the roots of the culture of hospitality that mandated showing all kindness to the newcomer, that ultimately unknowable being." Kapuscinski, Ryszard. "Encountering the Other: The Challenge for the 21st Century." *New Perspectives Quarterly*, vol. 22, no. 4, 2005, pp. 6–13. http://www.digitalnpq.org/articles/nobel/8/08-05-2005/ryszard_kapuscinski

[108] 1 John 3:17-18, New American Standard Bible.

[109] Buber, Martin. *I and Thou* (2d ed.). New York: Scribner, 1958.

[110] Milosz, Czeslaw. "Recovering a Reverence for Being." *New Perspectives Quarterly*, vol. 16, no. 3, 1999, pp. 4–9.

[111] "*How common is the lightning, / how lost the leviathans / we no longer look for!*" Walcott, Derek "Volcano." In *Collected Poems, 1948-1984* (New edition ed.). Farrar, Straus and Giroux, January 1, 1987.

[112] For more information, see NPR, George Monbiot, The Fragile, Invisible Connections of The Natural World September 28, 2013. http://www.npr.org/2013/09/28/227118003/the-fragile-invisible-connections-of-the-natural-world and TEDGlobal 2013 http://blog.ted.com/2013/06/11/for-more-wonder-rewild-the-world-george-monbiot-at-tedglobal-2013/

[113] *"All know that the drop merges into the ocean, but few know that the ocean merges into the drop."* – Kabir

[114] Regardless of whether one believes in God, we have a duty to take care of one another. Rabbi Abraham Joshua Heschel points out that the prophets of the Hebrew Bible didn't talk about miracles. Rather, they taught that God wanted us to care for the widows and orphans and those in need. The message of the prophets, says Heschel, is that *God needs us to make this world better.* Heschel, Abraham Joshua. *God in Search of Man: a Philosophy of Judaism.* Farrar, Straus and Giroux, 1999. See also "The Spiritual Audacity of Abraham Joshua Heschel - On Being." *The On Being Project,* https://onbeing.org/programs/arnold-eisen-the-spiritual-audacity-of-abraham-joshua-heschel/ Even if we do not believe in God, it can be argued that we still have an obligation to care for one another. Dr. Bernard Rieux, one of the principal characters in Albert Camus' *The Plague,* works in spite of fate and hopelessness to help victims of the plague, because of his atheism. If there is no God to protect us, reasoned Rieux, then it is up to us to help alleviate the suffering of others. Camus, Albert. *The Plague.* Translated by Stuart Gilbert, Random House, 1972.

Living Will

[115] While 90% of people questioned think they will become senile in old age, only 4% of people older than 64 experience it in its most severe forms, and less than 10% experience a mild form of dementia. Langer, Ellen J. *Mindfulness.* Da Capo Lifelong Books, 1989.

About the Author

In his writing and work with individuals and groups, **John "Sean" Doyle** is driven by his belief in the goodness of people, that there is beauty all around us, and that there is reason for hope. His essays and stories are invitations to inject a little more hope, affection and meaning into the world. They are about recovering a reverence for being and creating a culture of kindness.

A long time lawyer and psychology professor, Sean studied philosophy at Rutgers, received his Juris Doctorate from Loyola University-New Orleans, and his Masters of Applied Positive Psychology from the University of Pennsylvania. A husband and father of three, Sean lives and writes in North Carolina.

For more, or to reach Sean, please visit www.JohnSeanDoyle.com.

Made in the USA
Lexington, KY
23 September 2018